Quaaludes

DRUGS

Alcohol

Alzheimer's and Memory Drugs

Anti-Anxiety Drugs

Antidepressants

Barbiturates

Birth Control Pills

Botox® and Other Cosmetic Drugs

Cancer Drugs

Cocaine

Codeine

Crack

Date Rape Drugs

Ecstasy

Heroin

HIV/AIDS Treatment Drugs

LSD

Marijuana

Methamphetamine

Morphine

Nicotine

Opium

Peyote and Mescaline

Prescription Pain Relievers

Quaaludes

Sleep Aids

Weight Loss Drugs

■ DRUGS

Quaaludes

Justin T. Gass, Ph.D.

Consulting Editor
David J. Triggle

University Professor
School of Pharmacy and Pharmaceutical Sciences
State University of New York at Buffalo

CHELSEA HOUSE
PUBLISHERS
An imprint of Infobase Publishing

To my wife, Abby: Thank you for everything that you do for me. You mean the world to me and I am eternally grateful for having you in my life.

Drugs The Straight Facts: Quaaludes

Copyright © 2008 by Infobase Publishing

Chelsea House
An imprint of Infobase Publishing
132 West 31st Street
New York NY 10001

Library of Congress Cataloging-in-Publication Data
Gass, Justin T.
  Quaaludes / Justin T. Gass.
     p. cm. -- (Drugs: The straight facts)
  Includes bibliographical references and index.
  ISBN-13: 978-0-7910-8546-2 (alk. paper)
  ISBN-10: 0-7910-8546-5 (alk. paper)
  1. Methaqualone abuse. 2. Methaqualone. I. Title. II. Series.

  RC568.M45G37 2008
  615'.7821--dc22

                          2007044422

Chelsea House books are available at special discounts when purchased in bulk quantities for businesses, associations, institutions, or sales promotions. Please call our Special Sales Department in New York at (212) 967-8800 or (800) 322-8755.

You can find Chelsea House on the World Wide Web at
http://www.chelseahouse.com

Text and cover design by Terry Mallon and Keith Trego

Printed in the United States of America

Bang EJB 10 9 8 7 6 5 4 3 2 1

This book is printed on acid-free paper.

All links and Web addresses were checked and verified to be correct at the time of publication. Because of the dynamic nature of the Web, some addresses and links may have changed since publication and may no longer be valid.

Table of Contents

The Use and Abuse of Drugs
David J. Triggle, Ph.D.   6

1. An Overview of Depressant Drugs   8

2. What Are Quaaludes?   21

3. Past and Present Use of Quaaludes   31

4. The Neuroscience of Quaalude Use   44

5. The Physical and Psychological Effects
    of Quaaludes   54

6. Quaaludes in the Popular Media   67

7. Problems Associated with the Use
    of Quaaludes   73

    Notes   84

    Glossary   86

    Bibliography   89

    Further Resources   90

    Index   91

    About the Author   96

    About the Consulting Editor   96

The Use and Abuse of Drugs

The issues associated with drug use and abuse in contemporary society are vexing, fraught with political agendas and ideals that often obscure information that teens need to know to have intelligent discussions about these very real problems. *Drugs: The Straight Facts* aims to provide this essential information through straightforward explanations of how an individual drug or group of drugs works in both therapeutic and non-therapeutic conditions, with historical information about the use and abuse of specific drugs, with discussion of drug policies in the United States, and with an ample list of further reading.

The series uses the word "drug" to describe psychoactive substances that are used for **medicinal** or nonmedicinal purposes. Included in this broad category are substances that are legal—and some that are illegal. It is worth noting that humans have used many of these substances for hundreds, if not thousands of years. For example, traces of marijuana and cocaine have been found in Egyptian mummies, the use of peyote and *Amanita* fungi has long been a component of religious ceremonies worldwide, and alcohol production and consumption have been an integral part of the social and religious ceremonies of many human cultures. One can speculate about why early human societies chose to use such drugs. Perhaps anything that could provide relief from the harshness of life—anything that could make the poor conditions and fatigue associated with hard work easier to bear—was considered a welcome tonic. Life was likely to be, according to seventeenth century English philosopher Thomas Hobbes, "poor, nasty, brutish, and short." One can also speculate about modern human societies' continued use and abuse of drugs. Whatever the reasons, the consequences of sustained drug use are not insignificant—addiction, overdose, incarceration, and drug wars—and must be dealt with by an informed citizenry.

The problem that faces our society today is how to break the connection between the demand for drugs and the willingness of agents and organizations, largely in outside countries, to supply this highly profitable trade. This is the same problem we have faced since narcotics and cocaine were outlawed by the Harrison Narcotic Act of 1914, and we have yet to defeat it despite current expenditures of approximately $20 billion per year on the "war on drugs." The best weapon against any societal challenge is an intelligent and informed citizenry. The purpose of this series is to educate our readers so that they can make informed decisions about issues related to drugs and drug abuse.

SUGGESTED ADDITIONAL READING

Courtwright, David T. *Forces of Habit, Drugs and the Making of the Modern World.* Cambridge, Mass.: Harvard University Press, 2001. David T. Courtwright is professor of history at the University of North Florida.

Davenport-Hines, Richard. *The Pursuit of Oblivion: A Global History of Narcotics.* New York: Norton, 2002. The author is a professional historian and a member of the Royal Historical Society.

Huxley, Aldous. *Brave New World.* New York: Harper & Row, 1932. Huxley's book, written in 1932, paints a picture of a cloned society devoted only to the pursuit of happiness.

David J. Triggle, Ph.D.
University Professor
School of Pharmacy and Pharmaceutical Sciences
State University of New York at Buffalo

1

An Overview of Depressant Drugs

Mandy was in college. It was Thursday night; Mandy's weekend had started that afternoon when she and her friends gathered for their weekly night out downtown. They all started drinking as they normally do, but this time a friend passed her a pill that he referred to as a "wallbanger." She popped it, not knowing exactly what to expect. Initially, this pill had some of the same effects as a couple of beers— mild stimulation at first, which made her feel energetic, a little less anxious, and more confident around the crowd. Being a somewhat shy girl, she really enjoyed this newfound freedom. Soon enough, the "better" effects started to kick in. There was a feeling of pleasantness running through her head. She also began to feel slightly drunk, which was a feeling that she liked and was used to. Since she was not very fond of the taste of alcohol, she enjoyed simply taking a pill instead of drinking beer.

About two hours after she took the pill, she felt tingling throughout her body, which was followed by numbness in her legs. Although the stress from school, work, and her parents was now disappearing, so were other things like coordination and kinesthesia (the awareness of body position and movement). Now, Mandy could barely walk without the help of her friends. Once she lost feeling in her legs, the sensation moved up her body until she could barely feel her hand touching her face. She was now very uncoordinated and had lost the ability to walk in a straight line. Several hours after popping the pill, drowsiness had taken over her body and all she wanted to do was sleep. The next morning Mandy woke up with little recollection of what had happened the night before. The only telling sign of her experience with quaaludes was the black and blue little toe that she apparently fractured the night before and didn't remember. Only now was she beginning to understand why it was called a "wallbanger."

WHAT ARE DEPRESSANTS?

Anxiety and insomnia are disorders that have tormented millions of people, and treatment for these afflictions has been sought for numerous years. Drugs known as **depressants** (sometimes referred to as a *downers, sedatives,* or *tranquilizers*) are substances that slow down the normal function of certain parts or systems of the body, such as the brain and central nervous system (CNS). What's the benefit of slowing down these bodily functions? With the ability to apply the "brakes" to the brain's functions, researchers and doctors can treat certain disorders that are associated with overactivity of the brain. This includes such afflictions as anxiety (nervousness), tension, sleep disorders, stress, panic

Table 1.1   Common Depressants

Drug	Common Names	How It Is Taken
barbiturates	Amytal, Nembutal, phenobarbital, barbs, yellows	injected, swallowed
benzodiazepines	Xanax, Librium, downers, sleeping pills	swallowed, injected
flunitrazepam	Rohypnol, forget-me pill, roofies, roche	swallowed, injected
GHB	Gamma-hydroxybutyrate, G, liquid **ecstasy**	swallowed
methaqualone	Quaalude, Sopor, ludes, mandrex, quad, quay	swallowed, smoked, injected

attacks, and seizures. The many depressant drugs in use today are prescribed for these disorders, and the majority of them fall into two categories: **barbiturates** and **benzodiazepines**.

BARBITURATES

Barbiturates, such as Amytal and Nembutal, were used mainly for the treatment of anxiety and as a sleeping aid. These drugs have the ability to change the levels of certain chemicals in the brain that are associated with apprehension and restlessness. Once these drugs were tested and thought to be safe enough for use in humans, they were often prescribed by doctors who sought to treat individuals with these disorders. A variety of different barbiturates have been produced. They are grouped into categories based on how long their effects last (e.g., long-lasting vs. short-acting). Although these drugs are effective at treating certain afflictions, it was soon discovered that these drugs were also highly addictive and potentially life-threatening. During the late 1960s, addiction to barbiturates increased dramatically and it was soon realized that the addictive properties of these drugs far outweighed the medical benefits. Abusers of barbiturates showed physical signs, such as tremors, restlessness, and tension, whenever the drug was taken away from them. Barbiturate overdoses became more common as abuse of the drug increased. These drugs are very potent in their ability to slow down the functions of the brain. Some signs of overdose include slow breathing, altered coordination, and lowered blood pressure. Excessive amounts of these drugs may also result in death due to respiratory arrest.

The highly addictive properties of barbiturates have placed them under tight control. Due to their adverse effects on the body and high potential for abuse and overdose, they are rarely prescribed to treat disorders such as insomnia and anxiety. However, barbiturates are still commonly used to induce anesthesia (for surgery) and sometimes are used in the treatment of humans and animals who are prone to having seizures (epilepsy).

BENZODIAZEPINES

Benzodiazepines (also known as "benzos"), such as Valium, Librium, and Xanax, are used to treat anxiety, stress, and panic attacks. Benzodiazepines can also be used to treat anxiety in certain minor medical procedures, such as dental work. These drugs are similar to barbiturates in that they slow down the brain's function. However, benzodiazepines produce less harm ful bodily reactions when compared to barbiturates. Although overdosing on barbiturates is often life threatening because of their effects on breathing and blood pressure, benzodiazepines have side effects that are much less harmful and, thus, reduce the risk of a fatal overdose. Benzodiazepines, however, still have side effects that include drowsiness, loss of coordination, and impaired judgment, but these effects are less likely than the effects of barbiturates to fatally affect the user. Although benzodiazepines are considered to be safer than barbiturates, they still have the potential of being abused because they can still produce good feelings just like other abused drugs. Ultimately, this could lead to an addiction to this class of drugs.

OTHER DEPRESSANTS

There are other drugs, also considered depressants, which do not fall into either the barbiturates or benzodiazepines categories. These drugs include alcohol and marijuana, and they have the same effect of slowing down the activity of the brain.

Another nonbarbiturate depressant, known as **quaaludes (methaqualone)** was created in 1955. This drug produces effects similar to those of barbiturates and benzodiazepines in that it slows down the functions of the brain. Once the beneficial effects of methaqualone were established, it was hoped that it would be safer than barbiturates and have less potential for being abused. This drug was prescribed by doctors for the same reasons as barbiturates and benzodiazepines: to treat insomnia or anxiety, and for use as a sedative or muscle relaxant. However, although the nonbarbiturate methaqualone was initially considered to be less dangerous and more beneficial than drugs like Nembutal

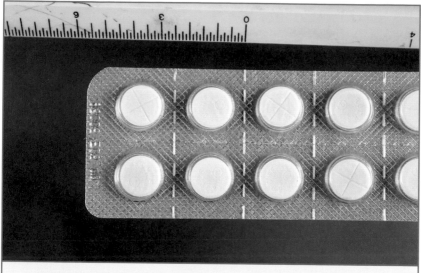

Figure 1.1 Rohypnol is a depressant that has become known for its use by rapists to incapacitate their unsuspecting victims. *(U.S. Drug Enforcement Administration)*

and Amytal, the addictive effects of methaqualone eventually began to outweigh its medical benefits.

GENERAL EFFECTS OF DEPRESSANT DRUGS

All of the drugs that are classified as depressants have the same general effect on the body and mind. The different drugs in this class each have unique effects, but they all produce feelings that result from slowing down, or sedating, the user's brain. Generally, smaller amounts of these drugs make a person feel more lively and relaxed. This stimulating effect can also occur with larger doses of the drug, but they occur only during the onset of the drug's effects, before the sedating effects begin. They may also produce a feeling of well-being and reduce inhibition. These feelings are similar to the feelings you get after a strenuous workout, after you've aced a difficult exam, or eaten a good meal. However, the effects of depressants are usually more intense. Once the user is relaxed and more likely to do things that he or she would not normally do sober, he or she may take more of the drug to continue feeling this way. If the user continues to take more of the depressant during the same episode of use, he or she will feel some of the most powerful effects of the drug.

Larger doses of depressants bring more intense, and even dangerous, effects to the user. A lack of concentration, probably due to fatigue, is a hallmark symptom of using depressants. The sedating effects of these drugs also significantly and adversely affect coordination—this effect is probably where the term *wallbanger* (slang term for quaaludes) comes from. In addition to sedating the actions of the brain, depressant drugs slow breathing and heart rate, as well as lower the blood pressure of the user. In extreme cases, the effects of depressants may cause the user to stop breathing (respiratory depression or arrest), which could ultimately lead to death.

The memory of the user can also be affected. Users may have little or no recollection of the period during which the drug's effects were at their peak. The memory-impairing effects of depressants can be harmful. For instance, some depressants, such as GHB and Rohypnol (roofies), are often used in sexual assaults. The victim may awake after the assault and have no memory that it even took place.

TRENDS IN THE USE OF DEPRESSANT DRUGS

Sedative drugs can be used for the treatment of many common disorders. Most of these drugs can be obtained from a pharmacy if a doctor prescribes them. However, these drugs also have effects that make them addictive, and people often take them for nonmedical reasons, or purposes other than those for which they are prescribed. According to a 2004 national survey on drug use, more than 6.3 million Americans reported that they were currently taking prescription drugs for nonmedical purposes.[1] This study indicated that, of these people, approximately 1.9 million used sedatives and tranquilizers. According to the same study, approximately 247,000 people tried illegal sedatives for the first time in 2005. This study also provided the average age at which a person first used an illegal sedative, which was approximately 23 years old.

Before they became illegal in the United States during the early 1980s, quaaludes were prescribed freely by doctors to treat anxiety and insomnia in the 1960s. However, during this same time quaaludes also became widely used recreationally by college and high school students. This was mainly due to the drug's intoxicating and euphoric (pleasurable) effects. During the 1960s, there was widespread rebellion to the Vietnam War and protests were common on college campuses. Taking drugs, including quaaludes, became part of the culture of rebellion. Soon the use of quaaludes increased when word of the drug's pleasurable effects spread. Quaalude use remained high during the 1970s, but dropped dramatically when the negative side effects became more apparent.

Sometimes the range of a drug's effects is not apparent until after it has been on the market for an extended period of time. If a drug has been through testing and is considered safe for human use, it will be introduced into the market. However, as the abuse of quaaludes increased, some of the potentially dangerous side effects, such as slowed breathing and addiction, became apparent in abusers. This prompted the government to weigh the medicinal effects against the drug's potential for abuse. Eventually, the potential harm that results from using quaaludes prompted strict control over its manufacturing and distribution. Quaaludes were then reclassified as a drug without medicinal benefits and a high potential for abuse, and thus, there was large decline in the use of the drug. The past and current use of quaaludes is explored more completely in Chapter 3.

Sedative drugs can be beneficial in treating certain disorders. However, issues of abuse and toxicity are associated with their use. Research has shown that there are generally two types of abuse that result from the use of sedative/hypnotic drugs.[2] The first is recreational abuse and the second is known as quasi-therapeutic abuse. Recreational abuse is associated with overuse of the drug mainly for the reason of getting intoxicated or high. These users typically abuse several different drugs at the same time (known as polydrug abuse) and are often young individuals. The method in which they take the drug is most likely oral, but sometimes they snort the drug. They usually take doses that are higher than the dose recommended by doctors. Their pattern of drug use can be **chronic** (repeatedly use the drug over a period of time), but most of the time, it is intermittent (not very consistent). Quasi-therapeutic use occurs when patients who once legally used the drug to treat a disorder begin to use (abuse) it in a way that is not approved by doctors. The characteristics of these users are different from recreational abusers. These abusers often take the drug as their doctor prescribes it, but often continue to take it even after the doctor advises that they stop taking the drug. They usually take the drug orally, but they continue to use the dose that was recommended by their doctor and often do not increase the dose above therapeutic levels. These users often obtain the drug through legal measures, but they may use deceptive procedures to get more of the drug when needed. An example of this would be having multiple doctors in order to receive several different prescriptions for the same drug.

HOW DEPRESSANTS AFFECT THE BRAIN

When considering how a drug works in the body, the first factor to examine is how it affects the brain. The brain is the most complex organ in the body. The complexity of the brain is what allows us to do such things as move our body, learn, form memories, write music and books, do arithmetic, sing, or do any of the countless other actions we perform on a daily basis. It also does things for us that we are usually not aware of, like controlling our breathing and heart rate.

The brain is part of the central nervous system, or CNS, which also contains the spinal cord. Overall, the brain consists of four different lobes (areas) that have different functions.

Although the brain only makes up about 2 percent of the body's total weight, it uses around one-quarter of the body's oxygen and nearly three-quarters of the body's glucose (carbohydrate that is used for energy). The brain works extremely hard and never goes to sleep. In fact, when your body is sleeping, the brain actually shows increased activity during certain periods of the night. Thus, it is easy to show how the brain is one of the most important and complex organs in the body. In addition to being involved in almost all of our behaviors, it is also the site of action for quaaludes and other drugs of abuse.

The brain is a well-protected organ. The skull protects the brain from injury. The skull is not the brain's only means of protection, though. The **blood-brain barrier** is a wall of tightly packed cells within the blood vessels near the brain that keep some harmful substances and chemicals from entering the brain. This barrier has certain doors that allow the brain to receive nutrients and oxygen from the blood. This barrier, however, is also responsible for letting certain drugs into the brain. Fat-soluble molecules such as oxygen, carbon dioxide, and steroids are allowed to pass through the barrier, whereas non-lipid molecules are not. Most abused drugs, however (including alcohol, caffeine, and quaaludes), have specific chemical structures that allow them to pass through the barrier and affect the brain. The crossing of this barrier is what permits drugs to act on certain brain areas and, thus, allows a drug user to feel the effects of the drug.

To understand how this process works, one needs to realize that the brain, like the body, is made of numerous cells—about 100 billion. The cells of the brain, however, differ from the cells outside of the brain and CNS. Cells in the brain are called **neurons**, and what makes these cells special is their ability to communicate with each other. A neuron is made of several structures, including the cell body, dendrites, axon, and synaptic terminal. Most neurons are arranged so that the end of one synaptic terminal is next to the dendrites of another neuron. The space between two neurons is known as the synapse, and

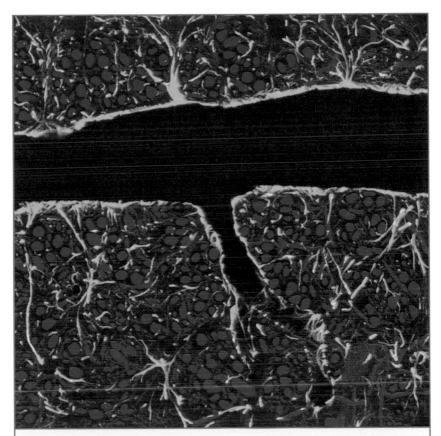

Figure 1.2 This confocal light micrograph image shows a blood vessel in the brain and the arrangement of cells that form the blood-brain barrier. When a drug passes through this barrier into the brain users feel the effects of the drug. *(© C.J. Guerin, Ph.D., MRC Toxicology Unit / Photo Researchers, Inc.)*

is an important part of the communication process. *Synapse* is the Greek word meaning "to clasp together."

Neurons communicate with each other by sending an electrical impulse (a process known as firing) that starts in the cell body and travels down the axon to its synaptic terminal. In the synaptic terminal, the neuron contains **neurotransmitters**, which are the chemical messengers of the brain. Once this electrical impulse reaches the synaptic terminal, there is a release of neurotransmitter into the synapse. On the other side of the synapse are the dendrites. This name comes from the Greek word for "tree branches." The purpose of the dendrites is to receive the chemical message (the neurotransmitters) from the neighboring neuron. They are essentially receptors for the neurotransmitter to bind with. Although there are many types of receptors on the dendrites, there are also different types of neurotransmitters that bind to those receptors. Certain receptors are shaped in particular ways, which allow only certain neurotransmitters to bind to it. In essence, there is a "lock-and-key" mechanism at the synapse, with the dendrites acting as locks and the neurotransmitters as keys.

It is important to understand how the brain functions under normal, drug-free conditions to understand the effects that drug use has on the brain. Communication between neurons, by neurotransmitters binding to their receptors, is an ongoing process. Once the neurotransmitters find their appropriate place on the dendrite, the receptor acts like an "on-and-off" switch for the next neuron. This means that if the message provided by the neurotransmitter is "fire," then the entire process begins again in the next neuron, with the creation of an electrical impulse in the cell body that is sent down the axon to the synaptic terminals. However, if the message delivered by the neurotransmitter is "do not fire," then the next neuron does not start the process. Although this process appears to be very simple, complex chemical and electrical reactions must occur for the message to be conveyed from one neuron to the next. With millions of neurons communicating with each other, the brain can tell the body to perform numerous behaviors and to feel many emotions. Although all of our behaviors, thoughts, and feelings are formed through very complicated actions within our nervous system, the simple act of neurotransmitters binding to their receptors is at the heart of it all.

Drugs are powerful because they can affect almost any part of this complex process. Just like a complex machine, neural communication requires that each and every component in the

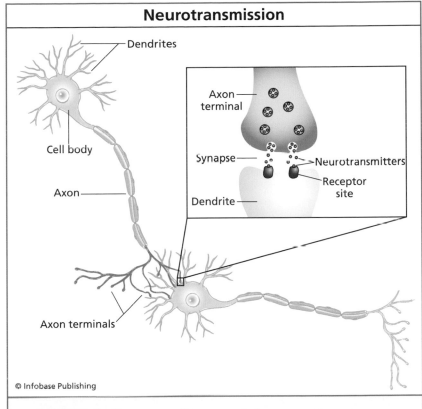

Neurotransmission

Dendrites

Cell body

Axon

Axon terminals

Axon terminal

Synapse

Dendrite

Neurotransmitters

Receptor site

© Infobase Publishing

Figure 1.3 Neurotransmitters move between neurons across a space called the synapse. (© *Infobase Publishing*)

process function correctly in order to have successful output. A malfunction at any point in this machinery can affect how well—or if—the machine works. With neurons, drugs can affect how the signal is communicated to the next neuron in several different ways. Drugs can interfere with the creation of neurotransmitters and the transportation of neurotransmitters from the cell body to the synaptic terminal. Drugs can also alter the number of receptors present on the dendrite or the amount of time the neurotransmitters remain in the synapse. The effects produced by drugs are a result of modifications in this process.

Recall that there are different types of neurotransmitters as well as different types of receptors. Different drugs have effects on different types of neurotransmitters and their receptors. Depressant drugs act primarily on the GABA (gamma-aminobutyric acid) neurotransmitter and receptor. GABA is the primary *inhibitory* neurotransmitter in the brain. When this neurotransmitter is released into the synapse and finds its way to the receptor on the dendrite of the next neuron, it is carrying a message telling this neuron "do not fire." Therefore, GABA inhibits the neuron from firing and can then depress the activity of that neuron, and countless others, under the proper circumstances. With an inhibitory effect, GABA plays a major role in both our movement and our arousal. Certain movement disorders such as Huntington's disease are associated with substantially low levels of GABA in the motor areas of the brain. With regards to arousal, low levels of GABA in the emotional centers of the brain can cause increased anxiety in some individuals. Thus, through their ability to increase the levels of GABA, it is apparent how depressant drugs can inhibit, depress, or slow down the activity of the brain and how this effect can be useful for treating disorders such as insomnia, anxiety, and panic attacks. These disorders are often associated with too much activity in certain areas of the brain. When properly used, depressant drugs can provide treatment by slowing down this overactivity. However, these drugs—quaaludes in particular—can also cause drunk-like, euphoric states in people who abuse them. It is for this reason that these drugs are dangerous and highly addictive.

What Are Quaaludes?

Robbie had just left his high school health class. There he had learned of the dangers associated with quaaludes. However, there was still one thing on his mind. Quaaludes are sedatives and they can be addictive, but why are they also used as medicine? He had learned from the Internet that this drug could be used as an antihistamine (for allergic reactions) and to treat coughs. They have names like lemons, mandies, and vitamin Q: what could be the harm in taking a quaalude or two just to relax after a hard day at school or football practice? Unfortunately for Robbie, his curiosity to experiment with drugs and the safe-sounding names of quaaludes would prove to be a dangerous combination.

Robbie was able to get a few quaaludes from one of his friends. So, one night, they decided to pop a few. Within 30 minutes, Robbie could feel tingling that began in his head and slowly spread to the rest of his body. There was also a rush of euphoria—he didn't have a care in the world. He felt like he was drunk, but without the fear of waking up with a hangover. The next morning, Robbie and his friend talked endlessly about how much they enjoyed quaaludes.

Robbie continued to take quaaludes at least once a week over the next few months. He noticed, however, that he had to take more of the pills to feel like he did during his first experiences with them. Also, the effects didn't seem to last as long. Now, not only did Robbie have to take twice the amount that he used to, but when the effects wore off, his body felt worse than it did before he took them. He didn't understand how quaaludes could make him feel so good at first and then make him feel so bad a few months later.

METHAQUALONE:
THE MVP IN THE QUAALUDE GAME

The major **psychoactive** chemical **found** in quaaludes is methaqualone (pronounced meth-ah-*kway*-lone). Although methaqualone is a highly addictive drug, it was originally created for medical purposes. It was discovered by researchers who were trying to develop a cure for malaria, an infectious disease. During the 1950s, there was a worldwide effort to reduce malaria—mostly in Africa, where the disease was most prevalent. In 1955, a researcher named M. L. Gujral developed methaqualone in hopes of creating a drug that would prevent and treat malaria. Although his attempt failed to help the fight against malaria, Gujral successfully created a drug that would soon become one of the most addictive—and **toxic**—sedatives in history. Once this drug was found to be ineffective for the treatment of malaria, methaqualone went through a series of tests to determine exactly what effects the drug produced. It was found that methaqualone tended to relax people and even make them sleepy. Initial research on this drug also suggested that it might be a non–habit-forming treatment for insomnia.[1]

Methaqualone is not classified as a barbiturate; however, it is structurally and functionally related to this class of drugs. The chemical name for methaqualone is 2-methyl-3-0-tolyl-4 (3H) quinazolinone. The chemical formula for this drug is written as $C_{16}H_{14}N_2O$, which shows that each molecule of methaqualone contains 16 carbon atoms, 14 hydrogen atoms, 2 nitrogen atoms, and 1 oxygen atom.

Methaqualone was originally prescribed to be taken orally. Thus, to make pills of this drug, white crystalline methaqualone powder is pressed into tablets (usually 150 to 300 mg) or simply put into capsules (dose range of 200 to 400 mg).[3] Moderate doses of methaqualone are usually considered to be around 150 to 300 mg, whereas high doses exceed 300 mg. Therapeutic doses are within the low-to-moderate dose range. Low and moderate doses of methaqualone tend to produce light sedation, relaxation, and drowsiness, whereas larger doses produce feelings of **euphoria** (intense pleasure), heavy sedation, depression, altered coordination, and slurred speech. Recreational users may begin with moderate doses; after repeated use, however, they must take higher doses to feel the same effects. Both the immediate and long-term effects of methaqualone use are covered in more detail in Chapter 3.

GENERAL FACTS ABOUT METHAQUALONE

Type of drug: depressant

How it is used: usually ingested as a pill, but can also be smoked

Onset of effects: around 30 minutes after ingestion

Duration of effect: around 4 to 8 hours

Physical danger: moderate to high (respiratory depression, cardiac arrest, convulsions)

Addiction potential: moderate to high

Source:[2]

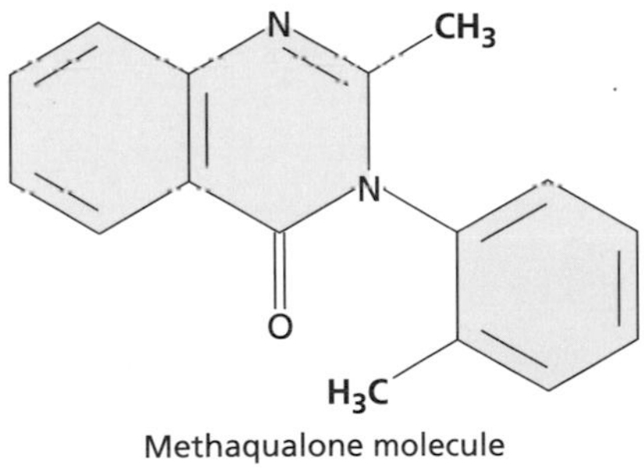

Methaqualone molecule

© Infobase Publishing

Figure 2.1   Methaqualone's chemical formula is $C_{16}H_{14}N_2O$.

THE HISTORY OF METHAQUALONE

Methaqualone was initially used for the treatment of several different disorders and was marketed under various brand names. Soon after its discovery in 1955, companies marketed the drug as therapeutic. Methaqualone was initially marketed in Europe and Japan as a sleeping pill. During this time, it was considered to be a nonaddictive **hypnotic** drug (a class of drugs that promotes or induces sleep). In 1960, methaqualone was sold by the Boots company under two different names, Melsed and Melsedin.[4] In 1965, Roussel Laboratories took a different approach to selling methaqualone. This company combined it with diphenhydramine, an antihistamine, and sold it under the name Mandrax. Combining methaqualone with an antihistamine probably enhanced methaqualone's ability to reduce the onset of allergic reactions.

Methaqualone was first marketed in the United States in 1965. The Rorer pharmaceutical company sold methaqualone under the name Quaalude. This name is now one of the most common and recognizable names associated with the drug. After seven years of being legally sold in the United States, methaqualone became the nation's sixth best-selling sedative drug. Given the popularity of this drug, a number of companies began to manufacture and produce methaqualone in an attempt to benefit financially from the legal use of the drug (as well as its abuse).

Table 2.1 Methaqualone's Many Names

Drug Company	Brand Name for Methaqualone
Parke-Davis	Parest
Carter-Wallace	Optimil
Arnar-Stone Laboratories	Sopor
Smith, Miller, and Patch	Somnofac

THE UNIQUE EFFECTS OF METHAQUALONE

Methaqualone has certain characteristics that are not common to other sedative drugs.[5] For instance, unlike other sedatives, methaqualone is **antispasmodic**. This means that it is a drug that can reduce smooth muscle contraction, essentially preventing muscle spasms of the stomach or intestines. Methaqualone can also be used as an **antihistamine**, which is a drug taken to reduce allergic reactions. Methaqualone also has the ability to act like cough medicine because it is able to reduce or suppress coughs, which makes it an **antitussive**. Finally, methaqualone can also be used as a local **anesthetic** to block the perception of pain.

Some users of methaqualone have reported that the drug can act as an **aphrodisiac**—an agent that increases or is thought to increase sexual desire. Thus, methaqualone has been referred to as a "love drug," which adds to its appeal among sexually active individuals. However, there is no conclusive evidence showing that methaqualone can increase sexual desire. Methaqualone may, however, act indirectly as an aphrodisiac through its ability to reduce inhibitions. Like alcohol, methaqualone can affect areas of the brain, such as the frontal cortex, that are responsible for controlling inhibitions. These areas help to control and prevent us from acting out some of our urges. Methaqualone can affect these areas by making us feel less inhibited and at the same time more relaxed and friendly. This can indirectly affect sexual desire by making us more likely to do things we would not normally do when sober. Based mainly on physiological findings, however, methaqualone actually reduces one's ability to perform sexually.

It was originally thought that methaqualone was an excellent alternative to barbiturates when used as an anesthetic during surgery. This was probably due to its usefulness as a muscle relaxant that did not produce severe effects on the respiration of the individual, under therapeutic doses. However, reports began to surface that methaqualone had the potential of being abused by patients who chronically used the drug, and it was withdrawn for consideration as an anesthetic agent. Nevertheless, the ability of methaqualone to reduce coughs, muscle spasms, allergic reactions, and its effectiveness as a sleep aid, added to the possibility that this drug could have extensive medicinal properties and be safer than other barbiturates that were currently in use.

Methaqualone also differs from other sedatives in the way that it affects the activity of the brain. For instance, using a technique known **electroencephalography** (EEG),

WHAT'S IN A NAME?

Why do drugs have terms or names that are different from their brand name? One of the main reasons that drugs have *slang* or *street* names is because they are illegal. When something is against the law in a certain society or culture, it is usually considered taboo (undesirable or unwelcome) in that society. One way to get around the taboo of drugs is to remove them from public awareness. This can be done by referring to the drug by names other than its brand name. In this way, the drug can be talked about freely within a particular crowd that understands the terms. Having slang terms for drugs is also a way of keeping the topic of conversation secret from authority figures such as parents or the police.

Methaqualone has many street and slang names. Although slang names are more common, methaqualone is also known by several trade names. Common street names: buttons (not to be confused with peyote buttons), down and dirtys, golf-sticks, gorilla biscuits, lemons, 714, lovers, ludes, mandies, mind peelers, Q, quad, quay, swastikas, vitamin Q, wallbangers, white pipe, whore pills, witpyp, and turkey gizzards. Methaqualone is also commonly known by previous trade names, such as Quaaludes, Sopor, Mandrax, Renoval, and Parest.

There is considerable intrigue surrounding the spelling of Quaalude. Although there are no clear facts on the scientists can measure the ways in which drugs alter a person's brain waves. These experimental studies have shown that methaqualone produces brain waves that are different from those produced by other sedative drugs,[6] indicating that methaqualone can affect the brain in ways that differ from other sedatives such as alcohol, Xanax, and Valium. This suggests that the unique medicinal effects of methaqualone may result from its ability to act on the brain in ways other sedatives are not able to.

subject, it is believed that there was special thought behind the unique spelling of the brand name. Essentially, spelling Quaalude with two *a*'s instead of one was done to create a positive response from the public. The company that used this name, Rorer Inc., also produced the best-selling product Maalox, which was named from the ingredients *ma*gnesium and *al*uminum hydr*ox*ides. In an effort to make their new drug, Quaalude, more recognizable among buyers, they decided to incorporate the *aa* spelling into the drug's name. It is also rumored that the name "Quaalude" is a combination of the words "quiet interlude," which most likely reflects the company's attempt to create a pleasant description of the drug's main effects as a sedative.

Quaalude has become an extremely popular name for methaqualone. Thus, these two names will be used interchangeably for the remainder of this book. Furthermore, "Quaalude" with a capital *q* refers to this brand-name drug, while "quaalude" with a lower-case *q* refers to the most common name for methaqualone as a drug of abuse. The next chapter discusses the use of quaaludes from their introduction in the 1960s to the present, when the drug is no longer considered to have any accepted medical use in the United States.

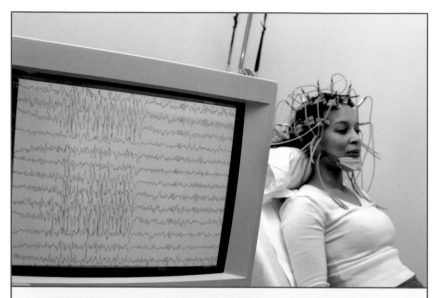

Figure 2.2   Electroencephalography (EEG) measures brainwaves and can be used to study how drugs such as methaqualone act upon the brain. *(© AJPhoto / Photo Researchers, Inc.)*

THE NEGATIVE EFFECTS OF METHAQUALONE

In addition to the normal subjective effects produced by depressant drugs, such as reduced anxiety, lowered inhibitions, impaired coordination, and memory problems, methaqualone also has some additional effects that are not common to other depressant drugs. For instance, methaqualone, when taken in amounts that exceed the therapeutic (moderate) doses suggested by a doctor, can produce states of euphoria. Although drugs from other classes are known to produce states of euphoria, methaqualone appears to be one of the few depressants drugs with this ability. Furthermore, this also makes methaqualone very dangerous, since people will repeatedly use the drug to feel this pleasurable state. This results in a greater possibility of methaqualone being abused and could possibly lead to addiction.

There are also health consequences of using methaqualone that differ from those associated with most other depressant drugs. Methaqualone can also produce effects that are opposite of euphoria. For instance, depression is a common side effect that occurs in individuals who have abused the drug and suddenly stop using it.

Methaqualone can also produce some immediate unwanted, or unpleasant, effects. Becoming dizzy, light-headed, and woozy are problems that are commonly reported by users. At the height of the drug's effects, methaqualone users may also feel weak and can be overtaken by feelings of paranoia and fear. Users often say that methaqualone makes them slur their speech and lose body coordination. One extremely dangerous characteristic of this drug is that users become **tolerant** to the effects quickly. When a person becomes tolerant to the effects of a drug, the amount of the drug that they have previously taken fails to produce the same effect. Therefore, the user must continually take larger amounts of the drug in order to achieve the same effects, or the same high, as before.

USING BRAIN WAVES TO STUDY ADDICTION

Electroencephalography is a technique in which scientists measure the electrical activity of the brain by putting electrodes on the scalp of a research subject. The electrodes measure the electrical signal that is produced in various regions of the brain. In other words, the brain waves that are produced can be measured from outside a person's skull. The brain waves are shown in an electroencephalogram (EEG) and indicate which areas of the brain are active during a particular time, such as when a person is exposed to a drug like methaqualone. Research from the UCLA School of Medicine in 2003 showed that drug addicts have brain activity that is similar to people with head injuries and memory problems such as dementia.[7]

A graph can be constructed to illustrate how tolerance to quaaludes can develop. This graph would show that while an abuser continued to take the same amount of quaaludes over an extended period of time, the effects or high that he or she experienced would decrease. Thus, the user would have to take more quaaludes to compensate for the development of tolerance.

METHAQUALONE, TOLERANCE, AND ADDICTION

Why is tolerance to a drug's effects important in addiction? Tolerance develops after the drug has been taken repeatedly over an extended period of time. What is interesting about tolerance is that the effect produced by the drug decreases during this time. In other words, the user would have to take more of the drug to feel the same high as before. For example, consider the use of methaqualone as a sleep aid. The repeated use of this drug every night to help with a sleep disorder would cause a rapid tolerance to its sleep-inducing effects. Therefore, the user would have to take more methaqualone each night to get the same sleep-inducing effects that he or she got the first few times it was used.

Tolerance does not only develop to the sleep-inducing effects of methaqualone. What makes the drug so dangerous is that users can develop tolerance to its euphoric effects. If a person continues to take methaqualone to get high, he or she must continue to use more of the drug to feel the same high that he or she felt previously. Methaqualone produces tolerance in a very rapid manner, which makes it a highly addictive drug. People who become addicted to drugs, including methaqualone, risk an **overdose** on the drug because they continue to increase the amount of the drug they take to obtain a particular high. Furthermore, tolerance might also develop for other sedative drugs. This is known as **cross-tolerance**. A methaqualone addict may have also developed tolerance to alcohol, benzodiazepines, or barbiturates, making this person prone to the addiction of not only methaqualone, but other sedatives as well.

3

Past and Present Use of Quaaludes

One of the main reasons Travis took quaaludes was because they were illegal; being told not to do something only fueled his desire to do it. Travis heard countless times from his parents, the police, the government, and the media that he shouldn't take quaaludes as a way to escape reality. What they didn't know, however, was that Travis wasn't taking them to deal with the stress of everyday life, but as a form of rebellion against all of the people that tried to run his life. He was old enough to make his own decisions. To make matters worse, Travis progressed from simply popping a few quaaludes a week to using them together with other drugs, like beer and pot, to really send the message to his parents that he was independent. Travis, however, failed to realize that combining these drugs was a life-threatening habit he shared with many addicts. Travis wasn't independent—he was addicted.

QUAALUDES: FROM MEDICAL USE TO ABUSE

Before quaaludes became illegal to possess or sell, they were often prescribed by doctors for several disorders. Thus, quaaludes became an extremely popular choice for people who were suffering from **insomnia** (sleeplessness) and **anxiety** (excessive worry). An immense advertising campaign launched by the large drug companies producing methaqualone targeted doctors in an attempt to increase sales of the drug.[1] In fact, these drug companies greatly benefited from this promotion: sales of the drug increased 360 percent in the early 1970s. Given that this drug was considered safe at the time by medical professionals, the legal use of quaaludes skyrocketed by people looking to cure their worries and sleepless nights. The increased use, however, also began to show the risks associated with using quaaludes.

Before quaaludes were available in the United States, Germany introduced methaqualone in 1960. They were sold without a prescription (over-the-counter). From 1960 to 1962, 10 percent to 22 percent of drug overdoses in Germany were associated with methaqualone use.   Germany was not the only country that experienced the negative effects of methaqualone before it was sold in the United States. Methaqualone was also introduced to Japan in 1960, and in the first four years that it was available, 40 percent of all drug overdoses in Japan were related to methaqualone abuse and misuse.

The problem of abuse was also widespread in the United States. Some reports showed that, a few years after quaaludes became available in this country, use was rampant on college campuses. For instance, one study showed that, during the late 1960s, 20,000 quaalude pills were consumed during a three-week period at Vassar College, and 5,000 pills were taken during a one-day period at Brooklyn College. Thus, only a few years after the introduction of quaaludes to the United States, use of the drug had escalated dramatically. With the increased abuse of quaaludes, there were more opportunities for the dangerous side effects of the drug to become apparent. Severe withdrawal symptoms, toxicity, and death from overdose were also common among heavy users.

In the early 1970s, as claims of the dangers associated with the misuse of quaaludes increased, the idea that this drug was safer than barbiturates came under question from doctors and scientists. In the United States, hospital emergency rooms began to see patients who had complications that arose from abusing quaaludes. For instance, patients were admitted for seizures and convulsions, and some went into comas. In 1974, quaalude overdose was responsible for 88 deaths in the United States. In 1976 and 1977 in the United States, an estimated 5,500 emergency room visits were associated with

Figure 3.1   President Richard Nixon *(center)* worked with his cabinet and the U.S. Congress in the early 1970s to create stricter drug laws, such as the Controlled Substances Act. *(© AP Images)*

quaalude abuse and its withdrawal symptoms. Despite the risk of dangerous side effects, quaalude use increased and quaaludes became one of the most abused drugs in the United States in the early 1970s.

Due to the widespread abuse of quaaludes, the United States Senate held hearings in 1973 regarding the legal status of methaqualone. These meetings resulted in strict control over the distribution and sale of methaqualone, which was achieved by classifying it as a Schedule II drug on the Controlled Substances Act. Schedule II drugs, although known to have an accepted medical use (such as treating pain), also have a high potential for being abused. Drugs classified as Schedule II carry certain requirements that must be met before a patient can obtain the drug. For instance, a person must get a valid written prescription (the prescription could not be phoned in) from a doctor and have the drug filled by a pharmacy.

WHAT IS THE CONTROLLED SUBSTANCES ACT?

In 1970, the United States government passed the Controlled Substances Act. This act categorized all drugs into five different schedules (classifications). These classifications were based on how medically useful, safe, and addictive a particular drug was.

The Department of Justice and the Department of Health and Human Services determine which drugs are added or removed from the schedules. Although there are currently five schedules, some states have added a sixth classification for substances that are not considered drugs in the typical sense, but are still abused. This classification includes a substance like toluene—a chemical found in many household cleaning agents that can be inhaled (huffed) to produce intoxication or a high. The drug classification schedules are as follows:

SCHEDULE I: The drug meets the following criteria: it has a high potential for abuse, it has no currently accepted medical use in treatment in the United States, and there is a lack of accepted safety for use of the drug or other substance under medical supervision. Examples of drugs in this class include heroin, methaqualone, cannabis, and peyote.

SCHEDULE II: The drug meets the following criteria: it has a high potential for abuse, it has a currently accepted medical use in treatment in the United States or a currently accepted medical use with severe restrictions, and abuse of the drug or other substances may lead to severe psychological or physical dependence. Examples of drugs in the class include morphine, amphetamine, and cocaine (which can be used as a topical anesthetic).

SCHEDULE III: The drug meets the following criteria: it has less potential for abuse than the drugs in Schedules I and II, it has a currently accepted medical use in treatment in the United States, and abuse of the drug or other substance may lead to moderate or low physical dependence or high psychological dependence. Examples of this drug include ketamine, buprenorphine, and anabolic steroids.

SCHEDULE IV: The drug meets the following criteria: it has a low potential for abuse relative to the drugs or other substances in Schedule III, it has a currently accepted medical use in treatment in the United States, and abuse of the drug or other substance may lead to limited physical dependence or psychological dependence relative to the drugs or other substances in Schedule III. Examples of drugs in this class include benzodiazepines, chloral hydrate, and some barbiturates.

SCHEDULE V: The drug meets the following criteria: it has a low potential for abuse relative to the drugs or other substances in Schedule IV, it has a currently accepted medical use in treatment in the United States, and abuse of the drug or other substance may lead to limited physical dependence or psychological dependence relative to the drugs or other substances in Schedule IV. Examples of drugs in this class include cough suppressants (containing small amounts of codeine) and some opium preparations used to treat diarrhea.

This classification is current as of 2007. Notice that methaqualone is now classified under Schedule I, rather than Schedule II. Florida reclassified methaqualone to this schedule in the early 1980s, and the rest of the United States soon followed. It is also interesting to note that nicotine, alcohol, and caffeine are not included in the Act. These drugs are some of the most abused in the United States. Furthermore,

(continues)

(continued)

there is no medical use for them and all are considered to be addictive, which are two characteristics that make them fit the criteria to be included in at least one of the schedules. However, alcohol and caffeine are generally considered socially acceptable, making it difficult to discourage their use. Additionally, alcohol and nicotine are taxed (and thus provide income for the government).

Also, the prescription cannot be refilled—another written prescription is required. The doctor who prescribed the drug and the pharmacy that supplied it must keep detailed records of its distribution. Additionally, the Controlled Substances Act mandates that pharmacies have to be registered with the Drug Enforcement Agency (DEA).

THE ABUSE OF QUAALUDES
IN OUR OWN BACKYARD

Even though methaqualone distribution was more tightly regulated by the federal government after 1973, use of the drug continued to escalate in various cities of the United States. The following information from the National Institute on Drug Abuse (NIDA)[2] reveals the extent of methaqualone use in several of these cities across the United States.

By 1979, quaalude use had been identified as the number one drug problem in Miami, Florida. Interestingly, only 1.6 percent of the treatment admissions in 1975 in Miami had been from methaqualone abuse; by 1979, this number had grown to 27 percent, suggesting that there was a rapid increase in its use within these few years. Similarly, 864 quaalude-related emergency room episodes were reported in Miami in 1979, compared to only 14 in 1975. The data also showed that quaalude use was highest in the young, white populations of Miami. In 1980, police in Broward County, Florida began testing the urine of intoxicated drivers and they found that 82 percent of them were on quaaludes.

During the early 1980s, quaalude use was very popular among junior and senior high school students in Atlanta, Georgia. During the same time, quaalude-related emergency room visits increased dramatically in Detroit, Michigan. In Hudson County, New Jersey, it was reported that quaaludes were readily available on the streets and cost less than 5 dollars. In 1981, quaaludes were the fourth most-confiscated drug in New Orleans, Louisiana. Similarly, in St. Louis, Missouri, quaaludes were one of the most readily available and popular drugs in the metropolitan area and were extremely popular among poly-drug users. In 1981, in Washington, D.C., quaalude-associated emergency room visits increased 30 percent from the previous year and continued to increase over the next two years.

These statistics suggest that quaalude abuse began in areas of the South, particularly the state of Florida. It then appeared to spread to states in the South that contained large cities, such as Georgia, Louisiana, and Missouri. However, quaalude abuse was also a problem in a few areas of the North, including Washington, D.C., New Jersey, and Michigan. Once quaalude production and distribution became more tightly controlled, abuse of the drug began to decrease in each of these states.

The classification of quaaludes as a Schedule II drug meant that a written prescription from a doctor was required to legally obtain the drug. However, users who were intent on obtaining these drugs devised ways around this. One of these methods included attending stress clinics. Beginning around 1980, these clinics provided an easy way to legally acquire a prescription for quaaludes. Stress clinics were staffed by doctors and counselors who were trained to provide treatment for severely stressed individuals. Patients would undergo a physical examination by a doctor and receive a stress-based survey from a trained counselor. If the patient was found to be stressed, the doctor would write a prescription for quaaludes. Legally obtaining quaaludes through stress clinics was not limited to extremely stressed individuals. Non-stressed people could imitate the signs and symptoms of a clinically stressed person and obtain a legal prescription for quaaludes. Some patients would keep the pills for themselves; others, however, would sell the quaaludes to make a quick profit.

People who were unable to attend stress clinics attempted to obtain quaaludes through different means. Thus, the illegal production of methaqualone increased dramatically. Many quaaludes were produced in **clandestine labs**, which are laboratories that secretly produce illegal drugs. However, most of the drugs produced in this type of lab are counterfeit, and it is difficult to know the actual purity and strength of a particular drug produced this way. The labs tend to be very efficient, and the equipment used to produce quaaludes has been shown to make in excess of 35,000 pills per hour.

The introduction of "juice bars" also made acquiring quaaludes much easier. These bars opened in Florida in the late 1970s and early 1980s. Juice bars simply consisted of people gathering to socialize and pop quaaludes. The name *juice bar* comes from the fact that juice was one of the only drinks available, presumably because most of the people attending were under the legal age to drink alcohol.

Although most of these bars only carried nonalcoholic juice drinks, there were some that had wine and beer. When a person uses both quaaludes and alcohol at the same time, it is known as "luding out." Both quaaludes and alcohol are depressant drugs, and when combined, can dramatically slow the functions of the brain. Luding out became very popular among college students for several reasons, which included easy access to quaaludes and alcohol as well as a tremendous amount of pressure from the college lifestyle. Using a drug in combination with another drug to alter the effects of each is not limited to

WHAT IS DRUG SYNERGISM?

The word *synergism* (synergy) comes from the Greek word *synergos*, which means "working together." This term refers to the ability of two or more substances (in this case, drugs) to work together to create an effect that is greater than the combination of the effects of each individual substance. In the case of drugs, taking two or more drugs at the same time can enhance the effects, including the side effects, of those particular drugs. Drug synergy has been shown with a variety of substances, including painkillers, antidepressants, depressants, and stimulants. For instance, using a combination of two antidepressants, doctors have been able to increase serotonin levels within certain areas of the brain. Depression is usually associated with decreased serotonin in the brain, and doctors are able to prescribe very specific combinations of antidepressants that have greater success in increasing serotonin levels than either of the drugs alone. Drugs that help with pain, like codeine, are often combined with other painkillers, such as ibuprofen, which serves to increase the pain relieving ability of codeine.

The synergistic effects of drugs, however, are also used for recreational purposes, such as to increase the high of a particular drug. One example of this would be cannabis (marijuana) and LSD (acid), which is a psychedelic drug that causes, among other things, visual and auditory hallucinations. It is thought that when these two drugs are combined, cannabis increases the psychedelic effects of LSD. Depressants, such as alcohol and Valium, act together to produce a strong depression of the brain's activity that is much greater than simply adding the individual effects of each one of these drugs. One potential danger of using depressant drugs in this manner is the risk of severely depressing breathing and heart rate, which could result in death.

methaqualone and can be found in the addictive patterns produced by numerous other drugs.

THE FALL OF QUAALUDES

Despite being classified as a Schedule II drug, quaalude use
continued to rise in the United States during the late 1970s
and early 1980s. Additional measures were taken by state
governments to control methaqualone manufacturing, and
the drug was classified as a Schedule I drug by the state of
Florida in 1982. Several other states followed suit during the
next few years, and in 1984 the federal government officially
classified methaqualone as a Schedule I drug. This meant
that the drug had a very high potential for abuse, that there
was no accepted medical use for treatment within the United
States, and that there was a lack of accepted safety for use of
the drug under medical supervision. This reclassification also
prohibited the manufacturing, distribution, and possession
of methaqualone. Most importantly, this classification made
methaqualone more difficult to obtain than it had been when
it was a Schedule II drug.

Additional tactics were used to ensure that quaalude use
would be limited. For instance, in the early 1980s agreements
were reached with most countries that produced methaqualone to stringently control the production and distribution
of the drug. Also, doctors began to prescribe methaqualone
only when the situation of the patient required it. Although
4 million prescriptions were written for the drug in 1973, the
number of prescriptions written in the early 1980s dropped
approximately 90 percent to around 300,000. Law enforcement
officials began to bust clandestine labs for illegally producing the drug. For example, in the early 1980s the DEA seized
57,173 kilograms of methaqualone, which could make 200
million tablets of the drug. Around the same time, the Federal Bureau of Investigation (FBI) busted a clandestine lab in
Miami, confiscating 3 million tablets, as well as the chemicals
used to make methaqualone.

Reclassifying methaqualone as a Schedule I drug had a huge impact on its illegal use in the 1980s. For instance, the use of quaaludes in Miami continued to decline, and only 11 percent of treatment admissions were primary quaalude users. In the early 1980s, San Francisco emergency room visits due to quaalude use dropped by 41 percent, whereas Los Angeles saw an 82 percent drop. Police data also show that there was very little quaalude use in Detroit by the mid-1980s. In 1995, the National Institute on Drug Abuse (NIDA) reported that there had been little methaqualone use in the United States in the decade spanning 1986 to 1995.

More recent data also show that quaalude use has declined. During the early 1990s, the DEA reported approximately 20 cases related to methaqualone use per year. A study from the United States Department of Health and Human Services showed that, between 2002 and 2004, about 3 percent of the adult population reported having used methaqualone for illegal purposes. However, this study also reported that the use of methaqualone among young adults was around 1 percent and use in youths was as low as 0.2 percent. These data indicate that since being withdrawn from the United States market, methaqualone use has faded and that, especially among younger people, use has become very rare.

This report also showed that while methaqualone was reclassified to Schedule I over two decades ago, in 2001 around 23,000 people started using methaqualone illegally. This shows that there is still a market, albeit small, for the drug in the United States. Most of the methaqualone found today comes from other countries such as Mexico. The majority of these drugs, however, are fake and illegally produced in clandestine labs. They are known as bootleg methaqualone and most likely contain sedatives that have similar effects to methaqualone. One report has shown that only 52 percent of these so-called quaaludes actually contained the drug methaqualone.

Counterfeit quaaludes often contain other drugs like painkillers (e.g., codeine), anesthetics, barbiturates

PRESENT DAY KNOCKOFFS OF QUAALUDES

During the 1990s, a drug with similar sedative properties to methaqualone appeared to have taken the place of the drug in the United States. Rohypnol, also known as roofies, was once referred to as the quaaludes of the 1990s. In a similar process to luding out, abusers of Rohypnol combine it with alcohol to produce sedating effects. Although it is currently a Schedule IV drug in the United States, many states are attempting to have it reclassified as Schedule I, due to its harmful effects and high risk of addiction, as well as its use as a date rape drug.

Another sedative, GHB, is becoming more widespread throughout the United States in cities such as Atlanta, Detroit, Miami, and New York, most likely due to its methaqualone-like effects. In fact, there is a combination of the drugs GHB, ketamine, and alcohol known as Special K-lude because it has similar effects to methaqualone.

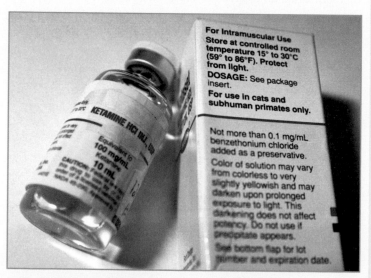

Figure 3.2 Ketamine is an anesthetic that can cause hallucinations; in combination with other drugs, it can produce a quaalude-like effect. (© AP Images)

(phenobarbital), and benzodiazepines (Xanax). It is difficult to determine the amount and purity of the drugs used in counterfeit quaaludes and, thus, these drugs can be very dangerous. Essentially, if the so-called quaaludes were mixed with certain substances that the user had not taken before (such as codeine), he or she may inadvertently take an excessive amount and risk an overdose. Additionally, the combination of different sedative drugs that may be present in the quaaludes could have a synergistic effect that may adversely affect the user's breathing and other vital functions.

Even though the illegal use of methaqualone has decreased dramatically in the United States since it was classified as a Schedule I drug, abuse of the drug is still a significant problem among adolescents in South Africa.[3] Most of the methaqualone found in this area is produced in local areas of South Africa and also different parts of Asia. In South Africa, methaqualone tablets are crushed and smoked with a mix of marijuana and tobacco in the neck of a broken off glass bottle. This combination is known as white pipe. Smoking methaqualone this way usually takes place in a group of people and immediately after inhaling the smoke, the users experience a short euphoria followed by a calm, relaxed state that may last up to six hours.

This chapter has shown how methaqualone has gone from a once-legitimate insomnia treatment to a life-threatening abuse drug. The public's perception of the drug's status is sometimes referred to as a "Dr. Jekyll and Mr. Hyde" story. This portrays how the public's initial acceptance of the drug progressed to a perception that it is an antisocial street drug when abuse skyrocketed and the addiction potential began to emerge.

4

The Neuroscience of Quaalude Use

Chloe didn't see much danger in taking quaaludes. The only thing she knew about them was that they made her feel funny and tingly. She thought that because quaaludes made her legs and arms feel strange, the drug didn't have effects on the rest of her body. She had no idea how drugs can affect the brain. She didn't know that quaaludes exert their effects on the body by changing the function of the brain cells, which are known as neurons. Certain receptors on these cells have the ability to slow down the functions in specific areas in the brain. When quaaludes enter the brain, they affect the entire body by reducing the activity of brain centers that control our movements, memory, inhibitions, and many other functions that are critical to our daily lives.

THE CHEMICAL MAKE-UP OF METHAQUALONE

The main psychoactive (brain-altering) substance found in quaaludes is methaqualone. It is a lipophilic (able to dissolve in fats, oils, and lipids), acid-soluble derivative of quinazoline.[1] It can be easily made from anthranilic acid, o-toluidine, and an acetylating agent. A few of the physical constants of methaqualone include its appearance, melting points, and solubility. Methaqualone is a white, crystal-like powder that has a melting point between 114°C to 116°C (in its freebase form). The freebase form of methaqualone is practically insoluble in water but is soluble in ethanol, ether, and chloroform.

Methaqualone is one of the most potent sedative compounds ever produced. This drug is not classified as a barbiturate, but it is structurally similar to other sedatives such as Doriden (glutethimide) and methyprylon. Doriden reached popularity just before the introduction of methaqualone. Like methaqualone, Doriden was thought to be a safer substitute for barbiturates, but also turned out to be extremely dangerous and addictive. The chemical formula for Doriden is $C_{13}H_{15}NO_2$, which is similar to methaqualone's formula of $C_{16}H_{14}N_2O$.

There are several different **analogues** of methaqualone. An analogue is a chemical substance that differs from its parent compound—usually by the addition or removal of certain molecules. When dealing with drugs, this results in a substance that has similar characteristics or effects to the original drug while differing slightly in chemical structure. A drug that has similar chemical characteristics to its parent compound will have a structure that has comparable elements (such as carbon and hydrogen) in its chemical makeup. For instance, drugs that have a chemical structure similar to methaqualone include other sedatives such as Doriden. With a similar chemical structure, Doriden can produce effects on the body that are similar to methaqualone's effects: sedation, loss of coordination, and relaxation.

HOW METHAQUALONE AFFECTS THE BRAIN

Drugs produce their effects by altering the transmission of neurotransmitters between neurons in the brain. Chemicals or substances that are taken into the body through various means, such as injecting, snorting, or ingesting, and then find their way into the blood. Through the blood they enter the brain. Once these chemicals reach the brain, they have the ability to cross the blood-brain barrier. Once they have crossed, they alter the function of neurons in certain regions of the brain.

Drugs alter the function of neurons by acting on the brain as neurotransmitters do: Some drugs bind to the receptors of neurotransmitters and mimic the action of the neurotransmitter, whereas others block the receptor and prevent the neurotransmitter from performing its job. Drugs can affect neurotransmitters in other ways. For instance, once a neurotransmitter is released into the synapse, there are processes that prevent it from staying for too long in the synapse. **Enzymes** (substances that speed up chemical reactions) break down the neurotransmitter, and **transport carriers** gather the neurotransmitter and move it back into the presynaptic

ANALOGUES OF METHAQUALONE

Several analogues of methaqualone have been produced in an effort to copy several of the medicinal effects of the drug. These analogues were produced with two objectives in mind. The first was to slightly change the chemical structure of methaqualone to produce a newer drug that would have similar medicinal value such as the ability to treat anxiety or serve as a cough suppressant. The second reason was to produce a newer drug that had the beneficial effects of methaqualone but produced fewer side effects. Experimentation with methaqualone's chemical formula has produced several different analogues; however, most of them were found to have as many side effects as methaqualone and thus are not currently being marketed.

The drug mecloqualone was designed to be faster acting than methaqualone, but it had a shorter duration of effects. Like methaqualone, mecloqualone was used to treat insomnia and anxiety. It was mostly produced in Europe during the 1960s. Cloroqualone, another methaqualone analogue, was also marketed in European countries, mostly during the 1980s, but more for its ability to treat coughs than for its sedative characteristics. Diproqualone, which was initially produced during the 1980s, also has similar effects to methaqualone, but this drug is used mainly for its anesthetic properties to treat ailments such as arthritis. Diproqualone is the only analogue of methaqualone that is used today for the treatment of pain—the others have been removed from the market due to their addictive and harmful effects and their potential for overdose.

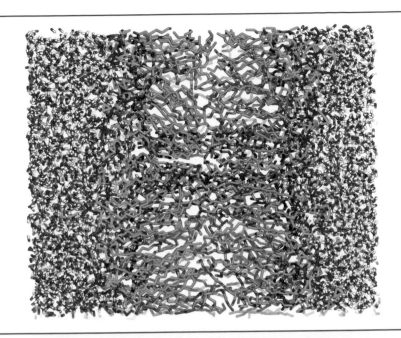

Figure 4.1 This is a molecular model of an ion channel. Ion channels are found in cell membranes, and allow the passage of ions into and out of a cell. Methaqualone inhibits the normal functioning of ion channels, causing sedation. *(© Laguna Design / Photo Researchers, Inc.)*

terminal. Some drugs decrease the activity of these enzymes or transport carriers, causing the neurotransmitters to stay in the synapse longer. Drugs may also affect neurotransmitter levels by changing the amount of it that is released by the presynaptic terminal. Finally, drugs may alter the function of the **ion channel**, or gate, located on a particular receptor—this is how methaqualone and many other sedatives work.

It is important to understand how ion channels function, since this is the basis for many of the effects produced by methaqualone and other depressants. Neurons contain several **ions**, such as sodium (Na), potassium (K), and chloride (Cl) that move in and out of the cell and control the cell's **membrane potential**, or voltage. When the neuron's potential is changed, depending on whether it becomes more positive or negative, the neuron will either fire (send a signal to the next neuron) or not fire (no signal is sent to the next neuron). The electrical signal that is sent to the next neuron affects the flow of ions and, thus, changes the membrane potential of that neuron. The entire process from the previous neuron is now repeated in the next neuron.

The ability of methaqualone to sedate this function of the brain results from its ability to change the function of the neurotransmitter GABA and its receptor. GABA is an inhibitory neurotransmitter in the brain. When GABA is released into the synapse from the synaptic terminal it binds to GABA receptors on the dendrites of the next neuron. When GABA binds to this receptor, it opens a channel, or gate, that allows Cl ions to flow into the cell. Cl ions enter the cell and change the membrane potential (voltage) of the neuron so that it becomes less likely to fire (or produce an action potential). By affecting this Cl channel (gate), GABA influences the neuron by inhibiting it from firing—this is why GABA is known as an inhibitory neurotransmitter.

Most sedative drugs do not produce their effects by changing the amount of GABA released from the synaptic terminal. Instead, receptors on the dendrites have specialized areas that allow the sedative drug to bind to it. When a sedative binds to this location, it increases the ability of GABA to open the Cl channel. In other words, sedative drugs help GABA open the Cl channel without opening the gate themselves. It is known that sedatives such as barbiturates and benzodiazepines have their own specialized location to bind with on the receptor. Although the exact way in which methaqualone affects the GABA receptor is not currently known, it is assumed that it too has a specialized location on the receptor that allows it to help GABA open the Cl channel and inhibit the neuron.[7] The result of this inhibition is essentially a slowing-down of the neuron. If a substantial number of neurons are inhibited, then certain brain structures may also be sedated. Thus, there may be an overall inhibition of the body and mind that could cause a number of effects, including deficits in body coordination, reduced anxiety, or relaxation. An excessive amount of sedation may result in respiratory depression and a decrease in functioning of the brain—both of which could be fatal.

Because methaqualone affects GABA transmission, it can have profound effects on the behavior of the user. This is because there are numerous GABA pathways in the brain. What is a brain pathway? The brain is made of several different regions that have different functions. For instance, areas of the brain stem control our breathing and heart rate, the amygdala is involved in our emotions, and the cerebellum

WHAT'S THE PURPOSE OF SPECIALIZED RECEPTORS?

Certain sedative drugs have a specialized location on the GABA receptor that only they can bind to. What is the purpose of this location and how did it get there? More than likely, the receptor is not there only to provide a place for drugs to work. Instead, substances are produced in the body (endogenous) that use these receptors. It is believed that the body can regulate certain conditions, such as anxiety, by manufacturing substances that bind to these areas and produce the same effects as the drugs used for these conditions. In other words, the body already produces "drugs" that can help control, among other things, our anxiety. Most psychoactive drugs of today, including both legal and illicit drugs, actually mimic substances that are already naturally occurring in the body. Most often, receptors for drugs are discovered after the drugs or certain neurotransmitters are found to bind with them; however, occasionally a receptor is discovered for which there is no known chemical substance that binds to it. Usually in such cases, scientists eventually determine what drugs and neurotransmitters bind to this receptor.

helps us coordinate our movements. Obviously, with so many different brain regions, we need a way for these different areas to connect with each other. A brain pathway consists of many interconnected neurons that allow one area to communicate with another. Since GABA is highly abundant in the brain, it is only logical that there would be several GABA-related pathways. For example, there are many GABA pathways located in the cerebellum. Most sedatives, including methaqualone, affect GABA transmission in the cerebellum, which is why these drugs often make the user feel uncoordinated.

HOW METHAQUALONE ADDICTION CHANGES THE BRAIN

Methaqualone, like other drugs of abuse, affects other neurotransmitters and pathways. Almost all abused drugs cause an increase in the neurotransmitter dopamine in an area of the brain known as the nucleus accumbens.[2] The increase in dopamine in this area is thought to be responsible for the euphoric effects produced by methaqualone and numerous other drugs. In other words, changes in the amount of dopamine in the nucleus accumbens cause the initial pleasurable effects of methaqualone that often lead to repeated use of the drug.

After abusing a drug for an extended period of time, a user can become psychologically and physically addicted to the drug. Briefly, the difference between psychological and physical addiction is based on the type of symptoms that are displayed by the user. For instance, a user is said to be physically addicted to a drug if he or she displays withdrawal symptoms. For instance, withdrawal from quaaludes produces symptoms such as tremors, insomnia, and anxiety. Someone experiencing withdrawal symptoms from quaaludes would be considered physically addicted to them. Psychological addiction is more associated with the wanting of drugs or the strong desire to use them. This type of addiction is not defined by the presence of withdrawal symptoms. Therefore,

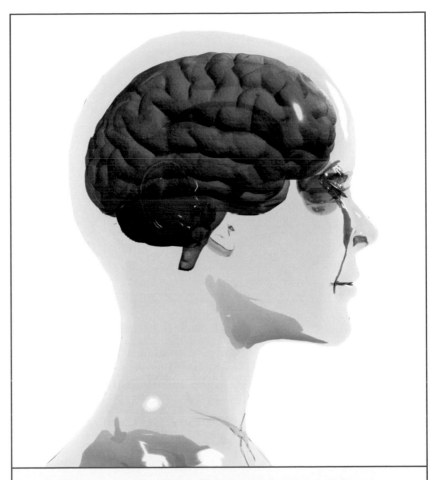

Figure 4.2   A computer rendering of the brain shows the cerebellum in red. Methaqualone affects GABA transmission in the cerebellum, causing users' movements to become uncoordinated. *(© Christian Darkin / Photo Researchers, Inc.)*

psychological addiction can still be present in someone who is not physically addicted to the drug and shows no signs of withdrawal symptoms. Psychological addiction is explained in greater detail in the next chapter.

Recent advances in scientific research, such as the ability to take images of the brain in living people, have shown that

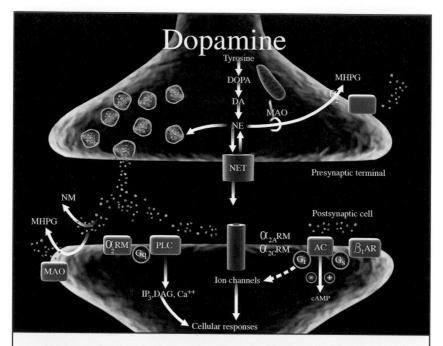

Figure 4.3 This illustration shows how dopamine flows during neurotransmission. Dopamine is involved with brain processes that control movement, emotional response, and the ability to experience pleasure and pain, and its levels can be affected by drug use. *(© Craig Zuckerman / Phototake)*

addiction results in drastic changes in areas of the brain that control our pleasure, motivation, inhibitions, and memory. In other words, the addicted brain is different from a non-addicted brain. Once a person becomes addicted, the prefrontal cortex, an area of the brain that is responsible for restraining or controlling our urges, is changed so that the addict is now less likely to control the desire to take the drug. Areas that are involved in memory, such as the amygdala and hippocampus, change in such a way that memories of the drug and its effects are very strong and often overwhelm the addict. An area closely related to the prefrontal cortex, the orbital frontal cortex, is responsible from motivating or driving the addict to find the drug. These are just a few of the many brain areas that are affected by repeated exposure to drugs such as quaaludes.

This chapter has shown how methaqualone can affect the brain. Unfortunately, many users of the drug fail to understand that methaqualone can, in addition to having sedative effects on the body, produce critical changes to structures in the brain. Chronic users of the drug may experience brain changes so drastic that they are unable to stop abusing methaqualone without medical supervision. Essentially, these individuals have become addicted to the drug.

5

The Physical and Psychological Effects of Quaaludes

Michael was hooked on quaaludes. He took them simply because they made him feel good. When he first started taking them, they made him feel calm, relaxed, and more sociable. When he would take more than usual, he started to feel intense pleasure. Michael continued to take quaaludes on a regular basis and found himself having to take more of the drug to get the same effects. Over time, Michael's behavior began to change dramatically when he was out of the pills and unable to find more. He was restless, irritable, and had difficulty sleeping. Sometimes, after Michael had taken large doses of quaaludes over a few weeks time and then stopped, he would have hallucinations—he would hear and see things that weren't actually there . . .

THE PHYSICAL EFFECTS OF QUAALUDES

Quaalude use can have a number of physical and psychological effects on the body. These effects depend on a number of factors, such as the amount of the drug taken, previous experience with the drug, and the method in which the drug is used. Depending on the amount of the drug taken, the physical effects can vary significantly. When quaaludes are ingested, the effects usually begin within 30 minutes and when a moderate dose is taken, the effects typically last 5 to 8 hours.

A low dose of methaqualone is considered to be around 75 mg, moderate doses are between 150 and 300 mg, and high doses are above 300 mg. The different doses of methaqualone produce different effects on the body. For instance, low doses of the drug produce changes in the body including drowsiness, fatigue, perspiration, restlessness, vomiting, and diarrhea. Moderate doses produce similar effects but are often more intense, like increased vomiting and drowsiness. The physical effects of methaqualone are most prominent at the highest dose of the drug. These effects include sleep (as opposed to drowsiness), muscle spasms (as opposed to restlessness), and rapid heart rate (as opposed to perspiration). The effects of high doses also include other serious concerns such as amnesia and severe respiratory depression.

Methaqualone and other drugs of abuse can produce noticeable effects on the body. The physical signs of intoxication can be used by police and authorities to determine if an individual is under the influence of drugs. Police officers use these signs to test for public intoxication and for tests of sobriety in people who are suspected of driving under the influence of alcohol. Thankfully, the police can use these physical signs to prevent harm to innocent individuals by drug users who attempt to drive and perform other activities while under the influence of drugs.

LONG-TERM PHYSICAL EFFECTS
OF QUAALUDE USE

The long-term physical effects of quaalude use differ from the short-term effects. One of the first long-term consequences of repeated methaqualone exposure is the development of tolerance. This includes tolerance to the sedative-hypnotic (sleep-inducing) effects of methaqualone, which become less effective with repeated use. Tolerance to the rewarding or pleasurable effects of the drug also develops quickly. A good example of tolerance is shown when users take two or three times the amount they initially used to produce a certain effect. New users to the drug may only need moderate doses of methaqualone (150 mg to 300 mg) to fall asleep or feel intoxicated. However, depending on the amount and degree of use (which will differ based on many factors such as gender, other sedative use, and expectations of the user), the

CAN YOU SEE INTOXICATION IN A PERSON'S EYES?

In addition to their psychological effects, such as pleasure and euphoria, drugs also produce effects on certain parts of the body. One of these effects is a change in the size of the pupils. Depending of the type of drug used, the pupil can either be constricted or dilated. Drugs such as barbiturates, codeine, heroin, morphine, opiates, glutethimide, and methaqualone cause the pupils to constrict, a condition known as miosis. Drugs such as amphetamines, cocaine, LSD, mescaline, and peyote cause the pupils to dilate, a condition known as mydriasis. Drugs such as GHB and PCP do not change pupil size but instead cause the pupils to move back-and-forth in a jerky fashion.

Doctors, drug counselors, and police officials use specified charts that contain illustrations of different sized pupils for use when examining a person suspected of being intoxicated. For instance, under normal lighting conditions, the pupil is around 3 to 4 mm wide. A chart held next to a person's eyes can be used for comparison. If the person's pupils are dilated to a size greater than normal, such as 7 to 8 millimeters, that person may be intoxicated with cocaine or other drugs that cause dilation. Similarly, if the person's pupils are smaller than normal, such as 1 to 2 millimeters, this could indicate that he or she is using methaqualone or addict may have to take as much as 1,000 to 2,000 milligrams to get the same high as before.

An experienced user of methaqualone is likely to experience **withdrawal symptoms** if he or she suddenly stops using the drug. Symptoms of methaqualone withdrawal range from mild to severe depending on the abuser's use and include things such as irritability, tremors, nightmares, and even seizures. Methaqualone withdrawal is covered in more detail in Chapter 7.

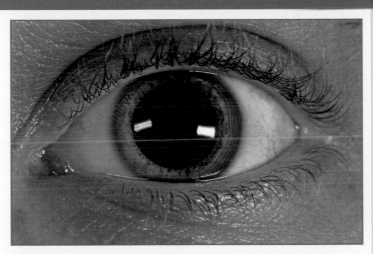

Figure 5.1 Mydriasis, or dilated pupils. *(© Frank Awbrey / Visuals Unlimited.)*

other sedative drugs known to constrict the pupils. Changes in pupil size, however, is not a foolproof means of determining that a person is intoxicated, it is only a physical side effect of using certain types and amounts of drugs. Many other things can cause a person's eyes to dilate or constrict, such as changes in room lighting and certain neurological conditions.

THE PSYCHOLOGICAL EFFECTS
OF QUAALUDE USE

The psychological effects of quaalude use differ from the drug's effects on the body because psychological effects tend to be the ones that users prefer. These effects, like the physical effects, depend greatly on the amount of methaqualone used, previous use of the drug, and the method in which it is taken. For instance, low doses of methaqualone (approximately 75 mg) give the user feelings of calmness and relaxation. Medium doses of methaqualone (150 mg to 300 mg) give the user feelings of euphoria and self-confidence. There is also a loss of inhibitions with this dose, which can be perceived as an increase in sexual arousal. High doses of methaqualone (over 300 mg) may, however, produce psychological effects that may not be preferred by some users. High doses of methaqualone can give the user perceived sensations of overall numbness of the body or even a fear of "losing one's mind."

A medium dose of methaqualone produces increased sociability. Like alcohol, the initial effects of methaqualone can actually create a slight sense of stimulation that is followed later by a more sedating effect. This slight stimulation makes the user feel more confident in social situations. This is why, like alcohol, methaqualone is a popular drug of choice at parties and other social gatherings. It is also worth noting that women tend to experience longer and more intense effects from methaqualone because women generally have a higher percentage of body fat than men, which results in larger amounts of the drug in the bloodstream.

ADDICTION VERSUS DEPENDENCE

People often use the terms *addiction* and *dependence* interchangeably, implying that the two terms have the same meaning. However, scientists have discovered that there are several different features of drug addiction. For instance, the psychological and physical effects of drugs are often associated with different components of addiction. The physical effects that occur when an abuser stops using the drug are displayed as withdrawal symptoms. The term *withdrawal* comes from the fact that the drug is being withdrawn, or taken away, from the abuser. When the user exhibits these symptoms, he or she is considered to be physically dependent on the drug. A physically dependent methaqualone user may display symptoms of insomnia or tremors when they are going through the withdrawal period.

The psychological effects of drugs, most notably the pleasurable effects, are more often associated with the term *addiction*. This is different from dependence because it refers to symptoms that differ from those displayed as physical withdrawal. Instead, addiction is defined as a compulsive, or obsessive, wanting of the drug even when there are severe consequences for getting the drug—such as harm to oneself or to others. In other words, addiction may be a form of dependence of the mind instead of the body. Methaqualone addiction would then be displayed as an intense craving for the drug instead of as physical withdrawal symptoms.

Scientists have shown that addiction and dependence are separate factors involved in the drug abuse process. This suggests that drug abusers could be (physically) dependent and/or (psychologically) addicted to a certain drug. A good example of the difference between the two is shown when addicts are treated in a rehabilitation facility until their withdrawal symptoms have disappeared. These addicts may still have an intense wanting of the drug even though the withdrawal symptoms are gone. Some doctors, however, do not make a distinction between these two aspects of drug abuse. However, an individual who is physically dependent on a drug needs to receive treatment that reduces the withdrawal symptoms. On the other hand, a psychologically dependent abuser requires treatment that eliminates the desire to take the drug. Since addiction and dependence are treated differently, it is important that this distinction be made because abusers need to receive the proper treatment.

THE EXPERIMENTAL DATA ON METHAQUALONE

When scientists study a particular drug, they must perform numerous experiments to determine the drug's effects on the body, its safety, and how it affects the brain. These studies are performed in both humans and animals. When a drug is developed, it must go through rigorous testing procedures for many years before it is actually produced for the public to use. Unfortunately, methaqualone failed to receive adequate testing before it was made available to the public. One reason for the lack of experimental testing of the drug prior to its release may stem from lack of concern for addiction in society. In the 1950s and 1960s, prescription drug addiction was not viewed as a significant societal concern. During that period, scientists were largely unaware of the significant brain changes and bodily harm that result from addiction to prescription drugs. Thus, there may not have been an overwhelming concern to test for the potential side effects of methaqualone prior to its introduction as a sleep aid. Thus, careful experimentation on methaqualone's side effects only occurred after the severe negative effects of the drug were reported.

One of the earliest studies on the psychological effects of methaqualone was conducted in the early 1980s by the University of Michigan Institute for Social Research, during the height of quaalude abuse. It consisted of a questionnaire given to 17,700 high school seniors that asked them to rate the degree (duration and intensity) of high obtained by quaaludes and compare it to other drugs of abuse. The results showed that although the intensity of the high from quaaludes was not as great as that produced by psychedelics (e.g., LSD), it had greater intensity than other popular drugs such as cocaine, marijuana, barbiturates, and alcohol. Thus, the perceived intensity of quaaludes is substantial since it ranks above other drugs, such as cocaine, that are known to produces highs of notable intensity.

The type of high produced by methaqualone has also been studied experimentally. For instance, it has been shown that subjects report the methaqualone high to be similar to that produced by Nembutal (pentobarbital), which is a short-acting barbiturate used for preoperative sedation, seizures, and as a sleeping aid.[1] When experimental subjects were asked to rate the high produced by methaqualone (200 and 400 mg doses vs. placebo) on several different scales including physical/mental sedation, euphoria/motor stimulation, and physical unpleasantness, the results showed that both doses of methaqualone were distinguishable from placebo on all scales. Also, both doses of methaqualone produced a similar euphoria but differed in their degree of sedation (e.g., the higher dose produced greater sedation than, but a euphoric state similar to, the lower dose).[2]

The pleasurable effects produced by methaqualone have also been compared to effects produced by Valium (diazepam), buspirone (a drug used to reduce anxiety), and a placebo. Volunteers were given each of these drugs for a week and then asked to rate the effects of the drug on a scale ranging from high to low. Methaqualone rated the highest on the scale of euphoria, stimulation effects, and estimated street value, whereas it placed second on the abuse potential scale, which asked whether the user would use the drug again. Other human studies have also shown that methaqualone use can have harmful effects on learning, sleep patterns, and driving skill. The ability of methaqualone to sedate functions of the brain are likely to cause deficits in learning, since the brain may not be activated sufficiently to form memories when under the influence of the drug. Additionally, the motor effects produced by methaqualone may severely hinder one's ability to successfully operate a car. The synergistic effects of methaqualone and other sedatives have also been validated in humans. For instance, in one study, methaqualone was shown to potentiate (increase) the sleeping time produced by several other sedative drugs, including alcohol.[3]

Research on the effects of methaqualone has not been limited to humans; it has also been performed on animals. Some of the earlier studies on this subject examined the physical effects of methaqualone. In rats, it was shown that repeated exposure to methaqualone caused a number of changes in the body. These changes include a decrease in body temperature, a decline in activity, and a decrease in body weight. When the same rats were withdrawn from methaqualone (the drug was taken away from them) they developed seizure activity—a sign indicating that the animals had developed withdrawal symptoms.

Methaqualone users often report changes in their motor skills when using the drug, and animal studies were developed to examine these changes. For instance, methaqualone administration caused rats and mice to lose their coordination and their ability to turn themselves over while on their backs (which is known as the righting reflex). The effects are more pronounced in dogs. A large dose of methaqualone caused dogs to lose their coordination, but soon after the administration, they become completely immobilized for close to eight hours, and they did not completely recover until 48 hours later.

Experiments in animals have also shown that there are differences between the sexes in the intensity of methaqualone's effects. In 1988, researchers in Tokyo, Japan, treated male and female rats with methaqualone at different doses by having it mixed with their food.[4] The results showed that female rats displayed decreased body temperature and impaired motor skills at the low dose, whereas male rats did not. Additionally, only the female rats also showed severe withdrawal signs (seizures and sometimes death) when administration at this dose of the drug was stopped. These results are similar to the human data showing that females are more sensitive to the effects of methaqualone.

Clearly there have been numerous studies showing that methaqualone can produce harmful effects in animals. The psychological (rewarding) effects of the drug have also been studied extensively in rodents and the data are just as convincing. One of the most used methods of measuring the

Figure 5.2   Lab animals, such as this rat, can be set up in a cage called a Skinner box. While inside this cage, the animal presses a bar to self-administer things such as food, water, or drugs. *(© Walter Dawn / Photo Researchers, Inc.)*

rewarding effects of drugs is the self-administration procedure. Basically, this test allows the animal to self-administer, or give itself, a drug by performing a task. This task usually consists of pressing a bar. The drug is then either injected into the animal's bloodstream or it is made available for the animal to ingest. This type of learning is known as **operant conditioning**. This form of learning is based on the consequences of one's actions. In other words, one's behavior can be modified if it has consequences, such as punishment or reward. Thus, the animal learns that if it presses a bar, it will be rewarded with a drug. Methaqualone is self-administered by animals, which reveals that the drug is rewarding to them just as it is in humans.

SELF-ADMINISTRATION IN ADDICTION STUDIES

The self-administration model is one of the most widely used procedures in the study of drug addiction. There are several reasons for its usefulness. First, it has **face validity**. This means that the procedure "looks like" or appears to accurately measure what it is intending to measure (in this case, drug addiction). Addiction in humans is characterized by voluntary use of the drug—it is not usually forced upon them. The self-administration procedure allows scientists to more accurately mimic addiction in humans by having animals show the same compulsive drug-taking. Second, it appears that animals will self-administer drugs for their rewarding effects, because almost all of the drugs that are abused by humans are also self-administered by animals. This means that animals will voluntarily give themselves most of the drugs that humans tend to become addicted to. This indicates that there must be some type of rewarding property that is inherent in abused drugs, since animals are naive about other influences on addiction, including expectations of drug effects and peer pressure. There are additional data that support the idea that animals will voluntarily administer drugs to themselves for their rewarding effects. For instance, humans rarely abuse some hallucinogens, such as LSD. One theory behind this lack of abuse is the idea that LSD does not produce extremely pleasurable effects (euphoria) like other drugs such as cocaine and heroin. Instead, LSD causes the user to hallucinate. Just like humans, when animals are given the opportunity to self-administer LSD, they will rarely administer the drug at rates that would reflect abuse or addiction.

Drug cues, which are stimuli that are repeatedly paired with drugs, are one of the main causes of relapse to drug abuse in humans. When addicts are presented with these cues, such as drug paraphernalia, they feel an intense craving for the drug. Using the self-administration procedure, scientists are able to pair certain stimuli, such as a light above the bar, with the effects of the drug. These stimuli then become drug cues and can be studied scientifically. Finally, any manipulation of the animal, such as providing certain medications, producing lesions to specific brain areas, or generating stressful stimuli, can be tested in the self-administration model to determine its usefulness in treating addiction. Some of the current medications used in addiction treatment were originally developed in studies that showed these medications could decrease operant responding (bar pressing) for the drug, presumably because the medication made the drug less rewarding.

There is a modification that can be applied to the self-administration procedure that allows it to measure the anxiolytic (anxiety-reducing) effects of a drug. In this procedure, animals are rewarded with a food pellet, instead of a drug, when they press the bar. Every few minutes or so, a light will appear above the bar, signaling that the animal can press the bar to receive a food reward. However, during the last few seconds when the light is on, the animal also receives a mild shock when it presses the bar. Usually, an animal will stop responding during this time. However, when the animal is given an anxiolytic (anxiety-reducing) drug prior to the session, they continue to respond regardless of the shocks. Presumably, the drug has made the animal less anxious about the anxiety-provoking shock. Research conducted at the University of Maryland in the 1980s has showed that not only does methaqualone produce euphoric effects, but it also contains anxiolytic effects that are similar to benzodiazepines because it will increase responding of animals during the punishment, or shock, periods in the experiment.[5] Thus, methaqualone is likely abused for both its euphoric and anxiety-reducing effects.

Data collected from human studies also shows the rewarding effects of methaqualone. Methaqualone is one of the most abused and toxic drugs in its class. The likelihood that a drug will be abused is known as its liability for abuse, and the unwanted toxic effects are known as the liability of abuse. In 2005, researchers at Johns Hopkins University School of Medicine performed a study that analyzed both of these aspects of abuse in methaqualone and in many other sedative/hypnotic drugs. This study showed that, among the 19 drugs used to treat insomnia, methaqualone ranked second highest in likelihood of being abused (liability for abuse) and third in level of toxicity (liability of abuse).

This chapter has explained the physical and psychological effects of methaqualone. Research has shown that not only is methaqualone a pleasure-producing drug, it also has physical effects that are both toxic and dangerous. Abuse of the drug often leads to addiction, and this fact outweighs the medicinal benefits of the drug. This is why methaqualone is classified as a Schedule I drug on the Controlled Substances Act.

6

Quaaludes in the Popular Media

Paul first heard about quaaludes through the music of his favorite band. The band wrote lyrics that reflected the band members' abuse of the drug and their experiences while using it. Thus, Paul thought there was very little harm in using quaaludes. If other people who used the drug can become as successful as the members of this band, Paul could certainly use them on the weekends without much harm. Unfortunately, Paul was influenced from the manner in which drug abuse is often glorified by celebrities and the media.

The glorification of drug use by celebrities is not a recent development. In the 1960s, many bands began experimenting with drugs in an attempt to "open up" their minds and attain a level of creativity that supposedly could not be reached in a sober state. Fans of these bands were also experimenting with drugs, both to experience this supposed increase in creativity and also as a form of rebellion. A great deal of this rebellion was based in opposition to United States involvement in the Vietnam War. During this time, drug use became an integral part of the music scene. Music festivals such as Woodstock provided an opportunity for attendees to experience the effects of illegal drugs with little surveillance by police officials.

The association of illicit drug use, influential music, and teenage rebellion strengthened during the 1970s. A variety of factors, such as easier access to drugs and the increased resistance to authority demonstrated by popular musicians, contributed to this association. Soon, drug abuse became almost synonymous with both the rock and roll lifestyle and teenage angst. References to drugs were common in popular music. Sometimes, these references were explicit, whereas in other cases the references were either metaphoric or hidden within the lyrics of songs. For instance, Rick James was a popular funk musician in the late 1970s and early 1980s—a period when quaalude abuse was high. James was known to experiment with many kinds of drugs, and he referenced quaaludes in one of his biggest hit songs. Instead of singing explicitly about the drug, he added a lyric to his 1981 song "Super Freak" that suggested use of quaaludes: "Room 714, I'll be waiting." The number 714 was a slang term for quaaludes that was popular at the time the song was released.

Although some rock stars chose only to sing about drug use and abuse, other performers, such as James, were actually referencing their own lifestyles through a musical outlet. These lifestyles often contained extensive drug use and bizarre or erratic behavior. Quaaludes had serious effects on several celebrities, although these harmful effects have usually been downplayed in the mainstream media. It is not difficult to find movies that portray quaaludes as a humorous, risk-free drug. For example, the Cheech Marin and Tommy Chong movie *Up In Smoke* portrays two drug users who play together in a band. This film debuted in the late 1970s and featured many quaalude references, which reflected the widespread abuse of the drug in the United States at the time. In fact, in addition to referencing quaaludes throughout the movie, Marin's onstage persona is named Captain Quaalude. Due to the popularity of this character, a Captain Quaalude toy figurine was later developed and marketed. Although this film was introduced decades ago, it still remains very popular, and special edition DVD copies of the movie are still being produced in 2007.

QUAALUDES AFFECT THE LIVES OF CELEBRITIES

Drugs, including quaaludes, have sometimes overwhelmed musicians and other celebrities. Celebrities often have the

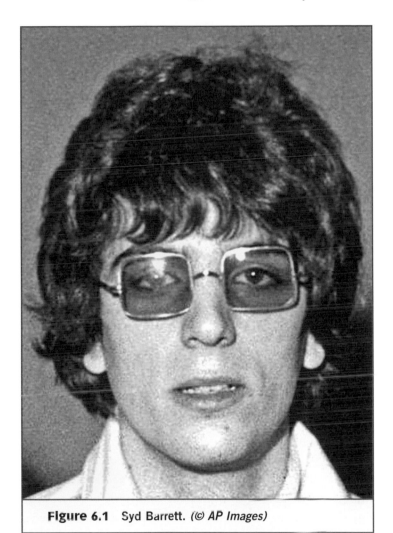

Figure 6.1 Syd Barrett. *(© AP Images)*

money and power to easily acquire large amounts of drugs and people who are willing to prescribe or provide them with drugs. The media's portrayal of the dangers of quaalude abuse has often been lacking or even lighthearted. This section contains a few examples of the serious and detrimental effects of quaalude abuse.

Syd Barrett was a singer, songwriter, guitarist, and one of the founding members of the rock band Pink Floyd. Barrett wrote much of the material during the early years of the band that eventually led to the band's critical acclaim in the late 1960s. Pink Floyd was well known for its psychedelic rock songs that fit well with the drug-influenced music scene at the time. Known as one of the creative geniuses behind the band, Barrett was also plagued by an addiction to drugs—most notably the sedative methaqualone and the psychedelic LSD. Barrett's preoccupations with the sedative eventually led to his use of the drug during his performances. Band members and fans have reported strange behavior on stage while he was under the influence of the drug. It has also been suggested that Barrett would combine large amounts of methaqualone with his hair gel before a show. During the show, the heat from the performance would cause the methaqualone-filled gel to melt and drip down his face, penetrating his pores, mouth, and eyes, and eventually finding its way into his bloodstream. Barrett was then able to feel the effects of the drug at the same time as his musical creativity was being rewarded by the presence of his fans. Barrett was also thought to suffer from mental illness, which could have possibly been triggered by or made worse by excessive drug use.

Anthony Kiedis is the lead singer for the popular band the Red Hot Chili Peppers. The band grew from a small Los Angeles-based punk rock band to one of the most well-known and influential alternative rock bands of today. Kiedis had a very untraditional childhood. Unlike most kids who were introduced to the dangers of drugs and sex by their friends, Kiedis was made aware of both of these vices from his father, who was a drug dealer. Even before the age of 13, Anthony's father had familiarized him with several drugs, including heroin, marijuana, and quaaludes. In fact, the night before his 12th birthday, Anthony's father gave him some quaaludes.[1] Kiedis has often noted that his early experiences with drugs such as heroin and quaaludes contributed to the severity of his heroin addiction as an adult.

Unfortunately, there have been several deaths of Hollywood celebrities that are methaqualone-related. Elvis Presley

Figure 6.2   Elvis Presley. (© *AP Images*)

was an icon of rock music. His status was so immense that he is still referred to as the "King of Rock and Roll." However, with all of the glory, money, and fans that were associated with being a rock star, Presley also experienced firsthand the troubles of drug abuse. Presley had difficulty adjusting to his stardom. The extensive touring and long hours of partying only fueled his need for drugs. His doctor made medications easily available. In fact, during the last two years of his life, Presley had received nearly 20,000 doses' worth of prescription drugs that included methaqualone and other sedatives, stimulants, and narcotics from his doctor. Presley eventually died from heart failure, which is believed to have been brought on by his addiction to a broad range of drugs, including methaqualone.

Freddie Prinze was the father of the now famous actor Freddie Prinze Jr. He was a famous television star in the 1970s during the peak of quaalude use in the United States. Prinze often abused methaqualone, which was provided to him by his doctor. Prinze was once arrested for driving under the influence of quaaludes, and he continued to battle addiction to the drug through the 1970s. On January 28, 1977, Prinze shot himself in the head and was taken to a nearby hospital, where he soon died. The initial cause of death was ruled a suicide, but the cause was later attributed to an accidental shooting resulting from intoxication of methaqualone.

This chapter has shown how quaaludes have affected the lives of several celebrities. The serious aspect of the drug, however, is often not reflected in the media, as quaaludes are often depicted as lighthearted fun. Unfortunately, this depiction undermines the overall fight against the abuse of quaaludes and other drugs. Certain media that portray quaaludes as harmless and fun may indirectly contribute to a teenager's curiosity about the drug, since the harmful effects of the drug are not shown. This chapter has shown how dangerous this misconception—and how damaging quaalude addiction—can be.

7

Problems Associated with the Use of Quaaludes

Christopher had tried everything he could to stop taking quaaludes. They used to make him feel good, but now he took them so he wouldn't feel bad. Christopher's friends began to notice that when he didn't take them, his personality changed. His muscles would twitch, his hands would shake, and he was very irritable, restless, and hard to get along with. Christopher even began to notice the withdrawal signs. He had to keep taking the drug to stop the symptoms. Even when they were not present, Christopher noticed that he had a strong urge to take more of the drug. His thoughts were completely consumed by the craving of the drug. Sometimes, all he could focus on was when and how he was going to get his next round of ludes.

Luckily, Christopher realized that he was addicted to quaaludes. He had taken the first step to overcoming his addiction. His parents and friends were able to find treatment for Christopher that consisted of detoxification, medication, and group counseling.

Christopher's story is one that was all too common during the height of quaalude use. Nowadays, widespread abuse of the drug is not a significant concern in the United States. The extent of quaalude addiction has decreased dramatically since it was reclassified as a

Schedule I drug and stopped being produced in the United States, but this decrease does not indicate that the drug is safe and unlikely to be abused. Even though drugs such as alcohol, cocaine, and nicotine currently receive the most attention from the media, the dangers of quaalude use and addiction are still present. The dangers of the drug are clearly seen in South Africa, where it is still highly abused. In fact, 85 percent of the world's methaqualone is consumed in this country.[1]

THE LIFE-THREATENING EFFECTS OF QUAALUDES

The dangerous effects of quaaludes are not limited to people who only take the drug to get intoxicated or high. Almost all sedative drug abuse has historically involved the oral use of legally manufactured medications. As explained in Chapter 1, there are usually two types of sedative abusers. The first is the individual who was prescribed the drug to treat a disorder (e.g., insomnia) but developed an addiction because of repeated use and misuse of the drug. Most often, these individuals fail to properly follow a doctor's orders on how often to use the drug. The second type of abuser is the individual who develops an addiction by repeatedly taking the drug to become intoxicated.

The dangerous effects of quaaludes can affect both types of abusers. One of the primary concerns with quaaludes, as with most depressant drugs, is the tendency of the drug to depress the rate of respiration. When a large enough dose of quaaludes is taken, breathing can stop. Even more dangerous are the synergistic effects of combining quaaludes with alcohol or marijuana, which significantly increases the chance of severe respiratory depression. Usually, the life-threatening effects of methaqualone use result from ingestion of large amounts of the drug. But when both methaqualone and alcohol are taken, the combined effects can occur even with small and moderate doses of methaqualone.

The life-threatening effects of methaqualone increase when the user is physically dependent on the drug. As the user

Figure 7.1 In addition to South Africa, India is one of the few places where methaqualone is still illegally produced. This Indian man has been arrested for trafficking the drug. (© *AP Images*)

develops tolerance, more of the drug is needed to get the same high as before. Thus, the user must continually increase the amount of methaqualone. Although the amount needed to get high increases, the amount of methaqualone needed to cause a fatal overdose stays the same. (For other abused drugs, such as heroin, the amount needed to kill an abuser increases as the person becomes tolerant.) Thus, the quaalude user will become closer to the fatal dose of the drug as he or she repeatedly increases the dose in order to get high.

The margin of safety of a drug can be quantified by dividing the amount needed to cause death by the amount needed to produce a small effect. Thus, a larger number would indicate an increased margin of safety. For methaqualone, a new user would experience a margin of safety around 14 or 15, whereas a dependent user would have a number around 2 or 3. The margin of safety for another sedative, phenobarbital, remains relatively constant between new and dependent users, which makes the effects of methaqualone unique within its class.

THE SIGNS OF WITHDRAWAL

The dangerous effects of quaalude abuse are clearly seen when dependent individuals stop taking the drug. When methaqualone is abruptly withdrawn, the initial symptoms appear within one to three days, and may last up to several days. The symptoms of withdrawal from the drug manifest themselves through disturbances in certain biological processes. There are a variety of symptoms common to methaqualone withdrawal, and they range from mild to severe. The extent of the withdrawal symptoms is usually based on how much methaqualone was abused. For instance, some abusers only use small to moderate amounts (approximately 75 mg to 300 mg) of the drug before stopping, whereas others abuse high doses (over 300 mg) and are severely dependent prior to the withdrawal period.

Withdrawal from light and moderate doses of methaqualone results in mild withdrawal symptoms. These include changes such as restlessness, irritability, insomnia, headaches, tremors, loss of appetite, nausea, abdominal cramps, and muscle twitches. A dependent individual may display a few or many of these symptoms. The withdrawal symptoms that occur after stopping heavy use of methaqualone are more severe. These include confusion, **delirium** (which is known as a deficit in attention, perception, and cognition), nightmares, **hallucinations** (sensory perception of sounds or sights that are not actually there), bleeding in the stomach, high fever, and seizures. The high fever and epileptic-like seizures can also be fatal to the individual.

One feature of withdrawal that is common to most abused drugs is rebound withdrawal. This occurs when a condition or symptom (e.g., insomnia or depression) that is present prior to the development of addiction—and sometimes initiates the drug use—returns when the drug is withdrawn. Usually, the rebound of this condition is more intense than before the

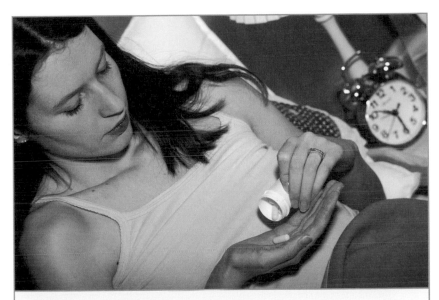

Figure 7.2 Quaalude addicts often experience insomnia as a withdrawal symptom. *(© AP Images)*

user began abusing the drug. Methaqualone was originally marketed to treat insomnia. Thus, when addicts that originally took the drug for this disorder develop withdrawal, they experience periods of insomnia that are more severe than the episodes they experienced prior to their addiction.

Recall from Chapter 4 that almost all drugs of abuse, including methaqualone, produce pleasurable effects through increasing the levels of the dopamine neurotransmitter in the nucleus accumbens. One key feature of the withdrawal process is the feeling of unpleasantness (known as dysphoria). This aspect of withdrawal is characterized by uncomfortable moods, depression, and irritability. Scientists have shown that dysphoria is associated with lower levels of dopamine in the nucleus accumbens, as well as an overall decrease in activity of this brain structure.[2]

When an excessive amount of methaqualone has been taken, there is a great risk of an overdose or toxicity from the drug. Toxicity, or poisoning, that results from high doses of methaqualone may lead to what is known as toxic psychosis. This is associated with severe delirium or hallucinations that usually goes away in a few days if intake of the drug is stopped. Other signs of toxicity or overdose include emotional instability and slow thought processes (mental signs), as well as stupor, vision impairment, and lack of coordination (physical signs). Toxicity to methaqualone can also cause hemorrhaging in tissue surrounding the eye, stomach, and intestines. The skin may also develop rashes, sores, blisters, or purple spotting from hemorrhaging under the skin. Furthermore, these individuals have a very fatigued look, which consists of a scruffy, messy, and unkempt appearance.

There are also more severe signs that may indicate an overdose from methaqualone. When an overdose has occurred, especially when luding out, the abuser can experience nausea, vomiting, and heavy saliva production. Furthermore, the user may have rapid changes in pupil size, severe heart rate depression, decreased muscle tone, decreased sensitivity to physical pain and loud noises, and even seizures. Ultimately, these symptoms may cause the user to fall into a coma, which is accompanied by extreme muscle rigidity.

Unfortunately, in heavily dependent users, death from overdose is likely because of methaqualone's low margin of safety. Overdosing can cause fluid to build up in the blood vessels, which leads to liver and kidney damage; this also leads to excessive body temperature, resulting in bodily shock. Death can result from failure of the lungs, kidneys, liver, or heart. Since methaqualone overdose does not affect a person's gag reflex, the user can also choke on his or her own vomit if it is inhaled.

TREATMENT FOR QUAALUDE ADDICTION

In the past, drug addiction was seen as a moral disease. Today it is known that addiction does not result from a person's lack of willpower to stop using the drug. Instead, there are numerous risk factors that can lead to addiction, including the genetic makeup of the individual, underlying mental health disorders, the age when abuse begins, home environment, and pressure from friends. Furthermore, research from the National Institute on Drug Abuse has shown that addiction is associated with substantial changes in the brain that prevent the abuser from quitting the drug. Drug addiction is now viewed as a disease, not a lack of moral strength. However, as cancer and similar disorders are diseases of the body, drug addiction is considered a disease of the brain. It can, however, be successfully managed with a variety of treatments by professionals.

Although there are several different methods of treating quaalude addiction, the outcome of these treatments depends

THE MANY WAYS TO DIE FROM METHAQUALONE

Death from methaqualone use does not only come from overdosing on the drug. During the height of methaqualone abuse, studies were performed that examined the deaths of people who used the drug. These studies revealed that after 1977, approximately three-quarters of all methaqualone-related fatalities were due to trauma or injuries that occurred while the person was intoxicated with the drug—only 17 percent were due to methaqualone overdose, whereas the remaining percentage died of causes that were not related to methaqualone misuse.

What these data show is that there are a number of ways one can be injured (or even die) from the use of methaqualone. Just like alcohol and other sedatives, methaqualone has severe effects on the motor abilities that affect one's capacity to do things such as drive a car, operate machinery, or perform other activities that require intact motor skills. Thus, it is not difficult to imagine the numerous behaviors that can become extremely dangerous while using methaqualone.

on a number of factors, such as addictions to other drugs, previous attempts at rehabilitation, motivation to engage in treatment, support from others during treatment, and ongoing involvement in other antisocial behaviors (such as gang-related activities).[3] Gender also plays an extremely important role in addiction. This is of particular importance when the abused drug is methaqualone, since addiction to this drug is most common among males. The age of the individual is also significant. Adolescents and young adults are the most prone to develop addiction. This is likely due to a variety of reasons that include peer pressure and degree of brain development; however, they are also the group most difficult to treat.

There are four general types of treatment commonly used for quaalude addiction: inpatient, outpatient, pharmacological, and psychosocial. Inpatient treatment programs consist of having the patient stay at the treatment facility (e.g., drug rehabilitation facility) for a specific amount of time (from 1 to 12 weeks) and, depending on the facility, includes a number of services, such as detoxification (process of gradually removing the drug from the body), group therapy, individual counseling, and aftercare services.

Outpatient treatment facilities are similar to inpatient services except that the individual only comes in during the day for treatment and returns home in the evening. Since a person receiving outpatient treatment is not monitored after leaving the facility, attendance is often inconsistent. The chances of maintaining a drug-free environment for patients is also very unlikely, since patients often return home to friends and places that were associated with their drug use.

Pharmacological treatments involve the use of medications that can help with the detoxification process and help maintain abstinence from the drug. This treatment is not simply substituting one drug for another. Instead, the drug used for treatment has different properties, such as a lesser high or a smaller range of effects. Thus, it is difficult for the patient to become addicted to the new drug, and, at the same time, allows the user to be withdrawn from the abused drug with minimal side effects resulting from withdrawal. This treatment can also be used in conjunction with other types of treatment, such as counseling.

Finally, psychosocial treatment regimens provide specific programs for the patient, such as the 12-step program, that help change the patient's view of addiction and their motivation to keep abusing the drug. The most successful treatment programs usually provide a combination of these different methods. Of course, there are other components to addiction that were not mentioned but are also part of treatment process. These include things such as financial, legal, and child-care services that assist the addict in improving various aspects of his or her life that have been affected by their disorder.

Individuals who are seeking help for quaalude addiction should never to try to quit the drug on their own ("cold-turkey"), because heavily dependent individuals who attempt to stop taking the drug can experience severe withdrawal symptoms. The severity of withdrawal in these abusers can result in death if not properly supervised. Thus, quaalude addicts should seek support from a medical professional who can monitor the user during the detoxification process and keep life-threatening symptoms controlled.

Currently, one of the best methods of treating withdrawal symptoms during detoxification is the use of pharmacological agents. These medications usually consist of drugs that have similar actions on the brain as methaqualone, but without the adverse side effects. Valium is the drug of choice for detoxifying dependent methaqualone users in South Africa. It may appear strange and even harmful to use drugs to help in the detoxification process, but this administration is strictly monitored by a medical professional to prevent an addiction to the medication. Although helping decrease the severity of the methaqualone withdrawal, Valium also helps reduce the addict's craving for quaaludes. The pharmacological effects of Valium are not nearly as potent as those of methaqualone. Valium does not produce the highly pleasurable effects that are common with methaqualone. Thus, individuals taking the medication are less likely to abuse the drug for its euphoric characteristics.

WHERE TO FIND HELP FOR METHAQUALONE ADDICTION

Clearly, quaaludes have many dangerous and life-threatening effects. Addiction is common with this drug. If you are abusing the drug, or suspect that someone you know is, it is critical to find treatment. The sooner that the addict begins to receive treatment for the addiction, the more likely the intervention will be successful. It is *not* true that addicts must first hit "rock bottom" before treatment can be helpful.

There are many Web sites available that provide information on how and where to start the treatment process. These include such sites as the National Institute on Drug Abuse (NIDA) and the Substance Abuse and Mental Health Services Administration (SAMHSA). The SAMHSA Web site provides listings for both public and private facilities in the United States that are licensed and certified to treat drug addiction.

It is also helpful to contact friends and family members of the individual who is having problems with methaqualone. These individuals provide support and may also know of professionals in the community who can help with the treatment process. Quaalude addiction is not an incurable disease, and—like other illnesses—it can be successfully treated with the proper care.

This chapter has shown the problems that are associated with the use and misuse of quaaludes. What was once viewed as a drug with valuable medicinal properties is now considered a highly addictive and potentially toxic drug.

Like many drugs of abuse, quaaludes can produce pleasurable states in abusers. However, repeated use of the drug results in a tolerance to its effects. The user must steadily increase the dose of quaaludes to feel the same effects, which increases the chances of an overdose. Compared to other abused drugs, quaaludes have a high risk of death associated with overdose. The lives ruined—or ended—by quaaludes have included Hollywood celebrities and everyday high school students. Although the possibility of addiction to quaaludes remains high, there are many resources available that can help treat addiction and abuse.

Notes

Chapter 1

1. Office of Applied Studies, "Patterns in Nonmedical Use of Prescription Drugs." Available online. URL: http://www.oas.samhsa.gov/prescription/Ch3.htm. Downloaded on October 24, 2006.
2. Griffiths, R.R. and M.W. Johnson, "Relative abuse liability of hypnotic drugs: a conceptual framework and algorithm for differentiating among compounds." *Journal of Clinical Psychiatry* 66, 9 (2005): 31–41.

Chapter 2

1. Ziemer, M. *Quaaludes. The Drug Library*. Springfield: Enslow Publishers, 1997, p. 112.
2. Gahlinger, P., ed. "Methaqualone and Glutethimide." in *Illegal Drugs: A complete guide to their history, chemistry, use, and abuse.* New York: Plume, 2004, pp. 351–358.
3. Carroll, M. and G. Gallo. "Quaaludes: The Quest for Oblivion." In *The Encyclopedia of Psychoactive Drugs, 2d ed*. New York: Chelsea House Publishers, 1992, p. 109.
4. Rudgley, R., ed. *The Encyclopedia of Psychoactive Substances.* New York: St. Martin's Press, 1999, p. 302.
5. Harvey, S.C., L.S. Goodman, and A.G. Gilman, eds. "Hypnotics and sedatives." in *The Pharmacological Basis of Therapeutics*. MacMillan: New York, 1975, pp. 102–135.
6. Brown, S.S. and S. Goenechea, "Methaqualone: Metabolic, kinetic, and clinical pharmacologic observations." *Clinical Pharmacology & Therapeutics* 14 (1973): 314–324.
7. Newton, T.F., et al., "Quantitative EEG abnormalities in recently abstinent methamphetamine dependent individuals." *Clinical Neurophysiology*. 114, 3 (2003): 410–415.

Chapter 3

1. Oakley, R., *Drug, Society, and Human Behavior*. 3d ed. St. Louis: C.V. Mosby Company, 1983, pp. 312–314.
2. National Institute of Drug Abuse. "Identifying and Monitoring Emerging Drug Use Problems." Available online. URL: http://www.nida.nih.gov/about/organization/CEWG/retro.html. Downloaded 2007.
3. McCarthy, G., B. Myers, and N. Siegfried, "Treatment for methaqualone dependence in adults." *Cochrane Database Syst Rev*, 2005(2): CD004146.

Chapter 4

1. Foltz, R.L., Fentiman, A.F., and Foltz, R.B. "Assays for Abused Drugs in Body Fluids." NIDA Research Monograph, 32 (1980): 39–50.
2. Baler, R.D. and N.D. Volkow, "Drug addiction: the neurobiology of disrupted self-control." *Trends in Molecular Medicine*. 12, 12 (2006): 559–566.

Chapter 5

1. Harris, L.S., "Problems of Drug Dependence 1989." NIDA Research Monograph. 95 (1990): 455.
2. Ionescu-Pioggia, M., Bird, M., and Cole, J.O., "Subjective Effects of Methaqualone." NIDA

Research Monograph. 95 (1990): 455.

3. Boissier, J.R., C. Dumont, and C. Malen, "Pharmacological study of a new hypnotic: 2-methyl-3-o-tolyl-4-quinazolone." *Therapie* 13, 1 (1958): 30–45.

4. Suzuki, T., Y. Koike, and M. Misawa, "Sex differences in physical dependence on methaqualone in the rat." *Pharmacology, Biochemistry, and Behavior.* 30, 2 (1988): 483–488.

5. Witkin, J.M., J.L. Katz, and J.E. Barrett, "Effects of methaqualone on punished and non-punished behavior." *Journal of Pharmacology and Experimental Therepeutics.* 218, 1 (1981): 1–6.

Chapter 6

1. Kiedis, Anthony. *Scar Tissue.* New York: Hyperion, 2005.

Chapter 7

1. Parry, C.D., et al., "Trends in adolescent alcohol and other drug use: findings from three sentinel sites in South Africa (1997-2001)." *Journal of Adolescence,* 27, 4 (2004): 429–440.

2. Heinz, A., L.G. Schmidt, and F.M. Reischies, "Anhedonia in schizophrenic, depressed, or alcohol-dependent patients—neurobiological correlates." *Pharmacopsychiatry,* 27, Suppl. 1 (1994): 7–10

3 McKay, J.R. and R.V. Weiss, "A review of temporal effects and outcome predictors in substance abuse treatment studies with long-term follow-ups. Preliminary results and methodological issues." *Evaluation Review.* 25, 2 (2001): 113–161.

Glossary

analogues—Chemical substances that differ from their parent compounds, usually by the addition or removal of certain molecules.

anesthetic—Having the ability to block the perception or feelings of pain; anesthetics are often used in surgical procedures.

antihistamine—Drugs that reduce the actions of histamines. Histamines cause allergic reactions; antihistamines relieve allergy symptoms.

antispasmodic—A drug that slows smooth muscle contraction.

antitussive—A drug used to reduce or suppress coughing.

anxiety—Unpleasant feelings of fear and worry.

aphrodisiac—Any substance that is known or believed to increase sexual desire.

barbiturates—Drugs that are used for the treatment of several disorders and that act as sleep aids, anti-anxiety drugs, and sedatives.

benzodiazepines—Drugs that are similar to barbiturates in that they can be used to treat anxiety and insomnia, but have fewer side effects.

blood-brain barrier—A barrier that allows certain substances to enter the brain from the bloodstream while keeping other substances out.

cannabis—Psychoactive substance also known as marijuana.

chronic—Persistent and lasting.

clandestine labs—Hidden laboratories in which secret illegal drug production takes place.

cross-tolerance—Occurs when a patient has repeatedly taken one particular drug (e.g., alcohol) and, when exposed to a new drug from similar class (e.g., Valium), shows signs of tolerance to the new drug.

delirium—A condition characterized by deficits in attention and cognition.

depressants—Drugs that slow down the function of the central nervous system.

ecstasy—A stimulant drug known to have hallucinogenic effects.

electroencephalography—Technique used to measure the electrical activity of the brain by placing electrodes on the scalp.

enzymes—Proteins that function to speed up chemical reactions.

euphoria—A state of intense joy or happiness.

face validity—The ability of a test to measure what it intends to measure and not a different concept.

hallucinations—Sensory perceptions, such as a sounds or sights, that are not actually present.

hypnotic—Class of drugs that has been shown to induce sleep or act as a sleep aid.

insomnia—Disorder characterized by difficulty sleeping.

ions—Molecules (or atoms) that have either a positive or negative charge.

ion channel—Pores located on receptors that allow the passage of certain ions into and out of the cell.

LSD—Chemical name is lysergic acid diethylamide, a psychedelic drug.

medicinal—Having the ability to heal; medicine.

membrane potential—The electrical potential or voltage of a cell, measured in millivolts (mV).

miosis—A condition in which the pupils of the eye shrink or become smaller.

mydriasis—A condition in which the pupils of the eye enlarge or become bigger.

neurons—The basic building blocks of the brain that are able to communicate with each other through electrical and chemical signals.

neurotransmitters—Chemical substances that enable different neurons to communicate with each other.

overdose—The result of taking more than the perceived recommended amount of a substance, usually a drug; may result in death.

operant conditioning—A form of learning in which consequences, such as punishment or rewards, are used to shape the behavior of an animal.

psychoactive—The ability of a chemical substance to alter the function of the brain and central nervous system.

quaaludes (methaqualone)—A drug originally thought to be a safe, effective treatment for insomnia and anxiety, but is actually a highly addictive sedative drug.

tolerant (tolerance)—Occurs when a person's reaction to a drug decreases and more of the drug is required to produce the original effects.

toxic—Having the ability to poison.

Glossary

transport carriers—Receptors used to catch neurotransmitters from the synapses and move them back into the presynaptic terminal.

withdrawal symptoms—Characteristic signs and symptoms that appear when an individual who has used a drug over a prolonged period of time suddenly stops using the drug.

Bibliography

Books

Carroll, Marilyn, and Gary Gallo. "Quaaludes: The Quest for Oblivion." in *The Encyclopedia of Psychoactive Drugs* 2d ed. New York: Chelsea House, 1992.

Gahlinger, Paul M. "Methaqualone and Glutethimide." in *Illegal Drugs: A Complete Guide to Their History, Chemistry, Use, and Abuse.* New York: Plume, 2004.

Harvey, Stewart C. "Hypnotics and sedatives." in *The Pharmacological Basis of Therapeutics.* New York: MacMillan, 1975.

Kiedis, Anthony. *Scar Tissue.* New York: Hyperion, 2005.

Oakley, S. Ray, and Charles Ksir. *Drugs, Society, and Human Behavior.* 3d ed. St. Louis, Mo.: C.V. Mosby Company, 1983.

Ziemer, Maryann. *Quaaludes.* Springfield, N.J.: Enslow, 1997.

Articles

Baler, R. D., and N. D. Volkow. "Drug addiction: The neurobiology of disrupted self-control." *Trends in Molecular Medicine* 12 (2006): 559–566.

Griffiths, R. R., and M. W. Johnson. "Relative abuse liability of hypnotic drugs: A conceptual framework and algorithm for differentiating among compounds." *Journal of Clinical Psychiatry* 66 (2005): 31–41.

McCarthy, G., B. Myers, and N. Siegfried. "Treatment for methaqualone dependence in adults." *Cochrane Database Syst Rev* 2 (2005): 1–8.

National Institute of Drug Abuse. *Principles of Drug Addiction Treatment: A Research Based Guide.* NIH Publication No. 99-4180. Printed October 1999.

Web Sites

National Institute of Drug Abuse. "Identifying and monitoring emerging drug use problems," NIDA.com Available online. URL: http://www.nida.nih. gov/about/organization/CEWG/retro.html.

Office of Applied Studies. "Patterns in nonmedical use of prescription drugs," United States Department of Health and Human Services. Available online. URL: http://www.oas.samhsa.gov/prescription/Ch3.htm.

Further Resources

Books

Gahlinger, Paul. *Illegal Drugs: A Complete Guide to Their History, Chemistry, Use and Abuse.* New York: Plume, 2004.

Hoffman, John, and Susan Froemke. *Addiction: Why Can't They Just Stop?* New York: Rodale Press, 2007.

Rudgley, Richard. *The Encyclopedia of Psychoactive Substances.* New York: St. Martin's Press, 1999.

Web Sites

Addiction Search
http://www.addictionsearch.com

The National Institute on Drug Abuse (NIDA)
http://www.nida.nih.gov

NIDA for Teens
http://teens.drugabuse.gov/

Partnership for a Drug-free America
http://www.drugfree.org

United States Drug Enforcement Administration (DEA)
http://www.usdoj.gov/dea/index.htm

abuse of drugs, 31–33, 36–38, 40, 65–66
acetylating agent, 44
acid, 39
addiction
  age and, 80
  dependence versus, 58–59
  gender and, 80
  to methaqualone, 30, 82–83
  psychological, 50–51
  self-administration in studies, 64–66
  treatment for, 78–83
age and addiction, 80
alcohol
  abuse of, 35–36
  brain waves and, 27
  depressant drug, 38, 39
  drug use and, 8, 31, 42, 74
  experimental data on, 60
  media attention, 74
  religious uses, 6
  sedative drug, 61
  stimulating effects, 58
  tolerance, 30
Amanita fungi, 6
amnesia, 55
amphetamine, 34, 56
amygdale, 52
Amytal, 9, 10. *See also* barbiturates
anabolic steroids, 35
analogues of methaqualone, 45, 46
anesthetic qualities
  of barbiturates, 10
  of cocaine, 34
  in counterfeit quaaludes, 41
  of methaqualone, 25–26
  preoperative, 61
  in treatment of arthritis, 46

anthranilic acid, 44
antidepressants, 39
antihistamine, 21, 24, 25
antisocial behaviors, 80
antispasmodic drug, 25
antitussive drug, 25
anxiety
  body's regulation of, 49
  buspirone use, 61
  measuring, effects of drug, 65
  treatment of, 9, 20, 31–32, 46
aphrodisiac drug, 25
appetite, loss of, 76
Arnar-Stone Laboratories, 24
arthritis, 46
Asia, 43
Atlanta, Georgia, 37, 42

barbiturates
  common depressant, 9
  in counterfeit quaaludes, 41
  described, 10
  effect on brain, 48
  effect on eyes, 56
  experimental data on, 60
  Schedule IV classification, 35
  tolerance, 30
Barrett, Syd, 69–70
beer. *See* alcohol
benzodiazepines
  anxiolytic effects, 65
  common depressant, 9
  in counterfeit quaaludes, 43
  described, 11
  effect on brain, 48
  Schedule IV classification, 35
  tolerance, 30
benzos, 11. *See also* benzodiazepines
bleeding, 76

blood-brain barrier, 16, 17, 45
body coordination, loss of, 29
bootleg methaqualone, 41
Boots company, 22
brain. *See also* blood-brain barrier
  -altering drug, 44
  decrease in activity of, 77
  depressant drugs effect on, 15–20
  effect of methaqualone on, 45–50
  function, 38
  methaqualone and, 50–53
  regions, 50
  waves, 27–28
Brooklyn College, 32
Broward County, Florida, 37
buprenorphine, 35
buspirone, 61

caffeine, 35
California, 41
calmness, 58
cannabis. *See* marijuana
Captain Quaalude, 68
Carter-Wallace, 24
celebrities and quaalude use, 68–72
central nervous system, (CNS), 9, 15–16
cerebellum, 50, 51
chloral hydrate, 35
chronic use of drugs, 15
clandestine labs, 38, 40, 41
Chong, Tommy, 68
Cl ion, 48
cloroqualone, 46
CNS. *See* central nervous system
cocaine
  euphoria and, 64

Index

found in Egyptian
mummies, 6
intensity of, 60
media attention, 74
pupil dilation, 56
Schedule II drug, 34
codeine, 39, 43, 56
cold turkey, 81
comas, 32
confusion, 76
Controlled Substances
Act, 33, 34–36, 66
convulsions. See seizures
cough suppressants, 35,
46
cramps, 76
cross-tolerance, 30
cues, drug, 64–65

DEA. See Drug
Enforcement Agency
death from methaqua-
lone/quaalude use, 32,
78, 79
delirium, 76, 78
dendrites, 18, 48
dependence versus addic-
tion, 58–59
depressant drugs
barbiturates, 10
benzodiazepines, 11
brain, effect on, 15–20
described, 9–10, 11–12
general effects, 12–13
synergism and, 39
trends in use, 13–15, 38
depression, 29, 39, 77
detoxification, 81
Detroit, Michigan, 37, 42
diarrhea, treatment of, 35
diazepam, 61
diproqualone, 46
dopamine, 50, 52, 77
Doriden, 44–45
downers, 9. See also ben-
zodiazepines; depres-
sant drugs
drowsiness versus sleep, 66

Drug Enforcement
Agency (DEA), 36, 40
drugs
classification schedules,
33, 34–36
cues, 64–65
legal/illegal substances,
6
margin of safety, 75–76
medicinal/nonmedici-
nal uses, 6
names, 26–27
recreational uses,
14–15, 39
synergism of, 39, 74
dysphoria, 77

EEG. See electroencepha-
lography
Egyptian mummies, 6
electroencephalography
(EEG), 26–28, 29
enzymes, 46–47
epilepsy. See seizures
euphoria, 23, 29, 43, 58,
61
eyes, intoxication effects
on, 56–57, 78

face validity, 64
FBI. See Federal Bureau
of Investigation
fear, negative effect of
methaqualone, 29
Federal Bureau of
Investigation (FBI), 40
fevers, 76
firing process of neurons,
17–20
Florida
GHB use in, 42
quaalude use in, 36–37
reclassification of
methaqualone, 35, 40
flunitrazepam, 9
freebase form of meth-
aqualone, 44
frontal cortex, 25

G, 9. See also GHB
GABA. See gamma-ami-
nobutyric acid
gamma-aminobu-
tyric acid (GABA), 20,
48–51
gamma-hydroxybutyrate,
9. See also GHB
gang-related activities, 80
gender and addiction, 80
Georgia, 37, 42
Germany, 32
GHB
common depressant, 9
effect on eyes, 56
sexual assault, use in,
13
widespread use, 42
glutethimide, 44, 56
Gujral, M. L., 22

hallucinations, 39, 42, 64,
76, 78
Harrison Narcotic Act, 7
headaches, 76
heart rate as physical
effect of methaqua-
lone/quaaludes, 55, 78
heroin, 33, 56, 64, 70, 75
hippocampus, 52
Hobbes, Thomas, 6
Hudson County, New
Jersey, 37
Huntington's disease, 20
hypnotic drugs
methaqualone, 24
tolerance to, 55–56
trends in use, 14–15

ibuprofen, 39
illegal drugs
clandestine labs and
production of, 38
medicinal and nonme-
dicinal purposes, 6
prohibition as reason
for using, 31
psychoactive, 49

slang and street names for, 26
strengthening of, 67
trends in use of, 13–14
India, 75
inhibitions, controlling, 25, 58
inhibitory neurotransmitter, 20, 48
inpatient treatment, 80
insomnia, treatment for, 9, 20, 31–32, 46, 74, 77
intestines, bleeding in, 79
ion channel, 47
ions, 47–48
irritability, 76, 77

James, Rick, 68
Japan, 62
Johns Hopkins University School of Medicine, 66
juice bars, 38

ketamine, 35, 42
kidney damage, 78
Kiedis, Anthony, 70
kinesthesia, 8
knockoffs of quaaludes, 42

legal drugs, 6, 33, 49
Librium, 9, 11. See also benzodiazepines
liquid ecstasy, 9. See also GHB
lipophilic quality, 44
liver damage, 78
lobes, brain, 15
Los Angeles, California, 41
Louisiana, 37
"love drug", 25. See also methaqualone
LSD, 39, 56, 60, 64, 70
"luding out", 38, 78
lung damage, 78
Maalox, 27
malaria, 22

mandies, 21, 26. See also methaqualone; quaaludes
Mandrax, 24, 26. See also methaqualone
marijuana
 celebrities' use of, 70
 experimental data on, 60
 found in Egyptian mummies, 6
 Schedule I drug, 34
 synergistic effects of, 31, 39, 43, 74
Marin, Cheech, 68
mecloqualone, 46
media, quaalude use in, 67–72
medicinal purposes for drug use, 6, 31–33, 36
Melsed, 24. See also methaqualone
Melsedin, 24. See also methaqualone
membrane potential in cell, 47
mescaline, 56
methaqualone. See also quaaludes
 abuse of, 65–66
 addiction, 30
 analogues of, 45, 46
 bootleg, 41
 brain changes and, 50–53
 celebrities' use of, 70
 chemical makeup of, 44–45
 common depressant, 9
 death from, 78, 79
 described, 11, 22–23
 effects of, 25–27, 65–66
 effects on brain, 45–50
 effects on eyes, 56
 experimental data on, 60–64
 freebase form, 44
 general facts, 23

history of, 24
illegal production of, 38
introduction of, 32
legal status of, 33
margin of safety, 75
negative effects of 28–30
other names, 24, 26–27
overdose, 77–78
Schedule I classification, 34, 35, 39, 40, 41
smoking, 43
source of, 41, 43
tolerance, 30, 75
toxicity, 65–66, 77–78
treatment for addiction to, 82 83
withdrawal symptoms, 50–51
methyprylon, 45
Mexico, 41
Miami, Florida, 36–37, 41, 42
Michigan, 37, 42
miosis, 56
Missouri, 37
moods, uncomfortable, 77
morphine, 34, 56
muscle spasms as physical effect of quaaludes, 55, 76
music, influential, 67–72

National Institute on Drug Abuse (NIDA), 36, 41, 79, 82
nausea, 76, 78
Neumbutal, 9, 10, 61. See also barbiturates
neurons, 16–18, 45, 48
neuroscience of quaalude use, 44
 chemical makeup of methaqualone, 44–45

Index

effect of methaqualone
on brain, 45–50
methaqualone and
brain changes, 50–53
neurotransmitters, 17–20,
45–48, 50, 52, 77
New Jersey, 37
New Orleans, Louisiana,
37
New York City, New York,
42
nicotine, 35–36, 74
NIDA. *See* National
Institute on Drug
Abuse
nightmares, 76
Nixon, Richard, 33
noise, sensitivity to, 78
nonprescription drugs.
See over-the-counter
drugs
nucleus accumbens, 50, 77
numbness, 58

operant conditioning, 63
opiates, 56
opium preparations, 35
Optimil, 24. *See also*
methaqualone
oral use of drugs, 74
orbital frontal cortex, 52
o-toluidine, 44
outpatient treatment, 80
overdose, 30, 77–78
over-the-counter drugs,
32

pain, treatment of, 46
painkillers, 39, 41
panic attacks, 20
paranoia,
Parest, 24, 26. *See also*
methaqualone
Parke-Davis, 24
PCP, 56
peyote, 6, 34, 56
pharmacological treat-
ments, 80–81

phenobarbital, 9, 43, 61,
75–76. *See also*
barbiturates
physical effects of quaaludes, 54–57
Pink Floyd, 69–70
placebo, 61
polydrug abuse, 15
pot. *See* marijuana
prefrontal cortex, 52
prescription drugs
nonmedical purposes,
13
refill, 36
written, 33, 37
Presley, Elvis, 70–71
Prinze, Freddie, 71–72
Prinze, Freddie, Jr., 71
psychedelic drug, 39,
60, 70
psychedelic rock, 70
psychoactive drug, 44, 49
psychological addiction,
50–51
addiction versus
dependence, 58–59
experimental data
on methaqualone,
60–64
quaaludes and, 58
self-administration in
addiction studies,
64–66
psychosis, 78
psychosocial treatment,
80, 81
punk rock, 70
pupils, size of, 56–57, 78

quaaludes. *See also*
depressant drugs;
methaqualone
abuse of, 31–33, 36–38,
40
celebrities' use of, 68–72
classification of, 34–36,
37
counterfeit, 41, 43

dangers associated
with, 32–33
depressant drug, 38
fall of, 40–41, 43
knockoffs, 42
life-threatening effects
of, 74–76
medicinal use to abuse,
31–33, 36
names for, 8–9, 13, 21,
24, 26
neuroscience of use,
44–53
physical effects of,
54–57
in popular media,
67–72
prescription, 37
problems associated
with, 73–83
psychological effects of,
58–66
schedule classification,
34–36, 37, 42
spelling of, 26
tolerance for, 55–56, 75
treatment for addic-
tion, 78–82
withdrawal symptoms,
32, 76–78
quinazoline, 44

rebellion, culture/form of,
14, 31, 67
rebound withdrawal,
76–77
receptors, 18–20, 45, 49
recreational use of drugs,
14–15, 39
Red Hot Chili Peppers,
70
rehabilitation, 80
relaxation, 58
Renoval, 26. *See also*
methaqualone
respiratory depression,
55, 74
restlessness, 55, 76

rock and roll lifestyle, 67–68
Rohypnol, 9, 12, 13, 42. *See also* flunitrazepam
roofies, 9, 13, 42. *See also* flunitrazepam
Rorer, Inc. (pharmaceutical company), 24, 27

saliva production, 78
SAMHSA. *See* Substance Abuse and Mental Health Services Administration
San Francisco, California, 41
schedule of drugs, 34–36
  Schedule I, 34, 40, 41, 66, 74
  Schedule II, 33, 34, 40
  Schedule III, 34–35
  Schedule IV, 35, 42
  Schedule V, 35
sedative drugs. *See also* depressant drugs
  brain waves and, 27
  described, 13
  effect on brain, 48–50
  methaqualone as best-selling, 24, 44–45
  oral use, 74
  physical/mental, 61
  tolerance to, 55–56
  trends in use, 13–15, 42
seizures, 10, 32, 61–62, 76, 78
self administration in addiction studies, 64–66
self-confidence, 58
serotonin levels, 39
sexual assaults, 13
sexual desires, 25, 58
shock, 78
Skinner box, 63
slang names for drugs, 26
sleep as physical effect of quaaludes, 55

sleeping pills, 9, 61. *See also* benzodiazepines
Smith, Miller, and Patch, 24
social stimulation, 58
Somnofac, 24. *See also* methaqualone
Sopor, 9, 24, 26. *See also* methaqualone; quaaludes
South Africa, 43, 74, 75, 81
speech, slurred, 29
steroids, 35
stimulants, 39
St. Louis, Missouri, 37
stomach bleeding, 76, 78
street names for drugs, 26
stress clinics, 37–38
Substance Abuse and Mental Health Services Administration (SAMHSA), 82
"Super Freak", 68
synapse, 16–19, 46–47
synergism, drug, 39, 74

teenagers
  addiction and, 80
  rebellion/angst, 67–68
therapeutic use of drugs, 14–15
Tokyo, Japan, 62
tolerance for methaqualone/quaaludes, 29, 30, 55–56, 75
toluene, 34
toxic drug, 22, 65–66
toxicity from methaqualone/quaalude use, 32, 77–78
tranquilizers, 9, 13. *See also* depressant drugs
transport carriers, 46–47
treatment for drug addiction, 78–83
tremors, 76
trends in use of depressant drugs, 13–15
12-step program, 81

UCLA School of Medicine, 29
United States, abuse of quaaludes in, 36–38, 40
University of Maryland, 65
University of Michigan, Institute of Social Research, 60
unpleasantness, feelings of, 77
Up In Smoke, 68
U.S. Department of Health and Human Services, 34, 41
U.S. Department of Justice, 34
U.S. Drug Enforcement Agency. *See* Drug Enforcement Agency

Valium, 11, 27, 39, 61, 81–82. *See also* benzodiazepines
Vassar College, 32
Vietnam War, 67
visual impairment, 78
voltage in cell, 47

wallbanger, 8–9, 13, 26. *See also* methaqualone; quaaludes
"war on drugs", 6
Washington, D.C., 37
Web sites on methaqualone addiction, 82
withdrawal symptoms, 32–33, 50–51, 57, 59, 76–81
witpyp, 26. *See also* methaqualone
Woodstock music festival, 67

Xanax, 9, 11, 27, 43. *See also* benzodiazepines

About the Author

Justin T. Gass received his bachelor's degree in psychology from East Tennessee State University. His graduate work was in behavioral neuroscience at the University of South Carolina (USC), Columbia. Dr. Gass received his Ph.D. from USC with a focus on drug addiction. He is currently a postdoctoral fellow in the Center for Drug & Alcohol Programs at the Medical University of South Carolina, Charleston, where he is supported by a training grant from the National Institute on Alcohol Abuse and Alcoholism (NIAAA). Dr. Gass is also adjunct faculty at the College of Charleston, located in Charleston, S.C.

About the Consulting Editor

David J. Triggle is a university professor and a Distinguished Professor in the School of Pharmacy and Pharmaceutical Sciences at the State University of New York at Buffalo. He studied in the United Kingdom and earned his B.Sc. degree in chemistry from the University of Southampton and a Ph.D. in chemistry at the University of Hull. Following postdoctoral work at the University of Ottawa in Canada and the University of London in the United Kingdom, he assumed a position at the School of Pharmacy at Buffalo. He served as chairman of the Department of Biochemical Pharmacology from 1971 to 1985, and as dean of the School of Pharmacy from 1985 to 1995. From 1995 to 2001, he served as the dean of the graduate school and as the university provost from 2000 to 2001. He is the author of several books dealing with the chemical pharmacology of the autonomic nervous system and drug-receptor interactions and some 400 scientific publications, and he has delivered more than 1,000 lectures worldwide on his research.